Green Eve

Don't Lose the Light Vortex

My Brain's Gone on Holiday~

Free Flowing Feelings

Sunny Jetsun

Krishnamurti:
"It is no measure of health to be well adjusted to a profoundly sick society"

* We have this Jewel Together *

Green Eve * Don't Lose the Light Vortex *
My Brain's Gone on Holiday ~
Free Flowing Feelings
*

Sunny Jetsun

Books by the Same Author:
Driving My Scooter through the Asteroid Field
Coming Down Over Venus ~ "Hallo Baba"
'Light love Angels from Heaven.
New Generation, Inspiration, Revolution,
Revelation ~ All the Colours of Cosmic Rainbows'
'Surfing or Suffering ~ together * Sense Consciousness
* fields of a body with streams and stars of hearts'
"When You're happy you got wings on your back ~
Reposez vos oreilles à Goa; We're only one kiss away"
'Psychic Psychedelic'
'Streaming Lemon Topaz Sunbeams'
'Invasion of Beauty *FLASH* The Love Mudras'
'Patchouli Showers ~ Tantric Temples'
'It's Just a Story ~ We Are All The Sun, Sweet Surrender'
Anthology #1 ~ 'Enjoy The Revolution'
Anthology # 2 ~ 'Love & Freedom ~ Welcome'
'He Lives In a Parallel Universe'
'Queen of Space ~ King of Flower Power ~ dripping Rainbows'
'All Love Frequency ~ In Zero Space'
*Peace Goddess*Spirit of the Field*The Intimacy Sutras*
'Heavenly Bodies ~ Celestial Alignments
Feeling ~ Energy that Is LOVE in Itself'
'I've been to Venus & back*These Are Real Feelings*
Let the Universe Guide Your Heart * through Space'
The Kiss in Slaughterhouse 6

Books by the Same Author:
Originally Published as Ciel Rose
'Sadhu Sadhu Sadhu ~ "All Beings Be Happy" ~ Shanti Shanti'
'Trilogy of Vibrations ~ The Oneness of Life'
'Each Fragment of Life Is Sacred ~ These Are Your Children'
'Young Women Spin On Their Doorsteps At Dusk'
'Life Is Simple, Sharing ~ Loving Kindness from the Heart'
'The Universe Coming Across the River'
*

Originally Published as Sunny Revareva
'Pure Light, Cosmic*Sweet Heart ~ We've All Got Stars Inside'
'Perfect Love ~ No Mind * Star Light ~ Come Alive'
'True Freedom ~ Natural Spiritual Beauty ~
Here * Now ~ Gems of Eternity'
***

This book is arranged from Surreal notes made from ~
Inspirational conversations with friends during the 2006/07
winter season in Anjuna, Goa ☺ "Thank you all" Om Shanti.

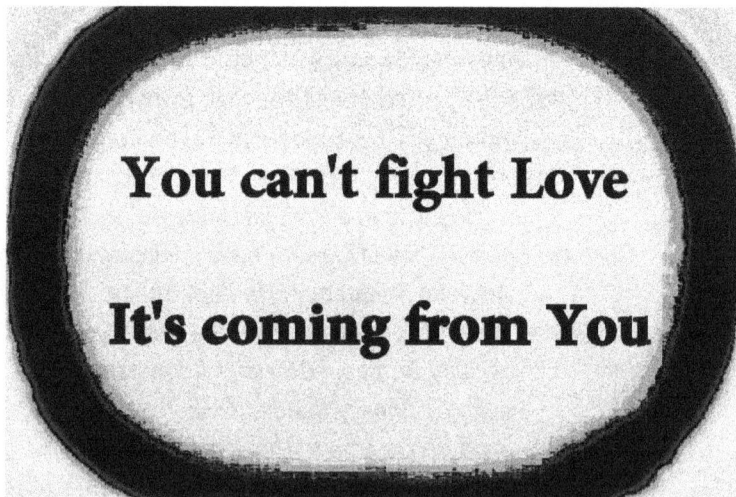

You can't fight Love

It's coming from You

BG: 'The Bhagavad Gita', A. C. Bhaktivedanta Swami Prabhupada*oa*

<u>We're All Stardust ~ This body is our Temple</u>
What is Really out there * Space, Known, Unknown & yet
to be discovered of our 'Human Condition' ~ this Fantastic
realisation that we're from a Quantum, infinite Cosmos
We now have a New concept of how to view, evaluate,
react, believe, having a relationship with our*Selves here!
Who are we, where are we from, where are we going?
Is it all in our genes that were always evolving into existence,
we just didn't know it! This is true of Unimaginable states still
to be found as we continue consciously on our eternal journey
as sub*atomical dimensions of Energy, Psyche, Mind, Identity,
Conditionings, Programming, Memories, fractal patterns of ego.
Karma ~ Our 'dis/orders', endless, awareness to be witnessed!
How to transmit a 'Universal concept' into a 'human' Sense?
How do we seem to have progressed so far, Signor Galileo?
Krishna says to grief stricken Arjuna on a bloody battlefield,
"While speaking learned words you are mourning
for what is not worthy of grief. Those who are wise
lament neither for the living nor the dead." (BG.ch. 2.11).
How/what is this Realisation based on? He teaches that essential
Knowledge is witnessing the difference between Materialistic and
the Non-materialistic, Spiritualistic phenomena ~ being here now
*

Realising this is a Sense Conscious body of boundless energy ~
caught by an Ignorant, false Ego, thinking Mind, creating '**FORM**'.
All sorts of Attachments, delusions, illusions (Maya,) trapping us.
We condition our Selves and are conditioned by other forces.
Our bodies & Minds working in energetic fields manifesting
'<u>disorders</u>' are not 'normal' to society so deemed '<u>Anti</u>' to it.
They fit you in their box to treat; You live in that box or not.
How would you ever have any idea, clue to transcend the box
you're told you belong in? And others will never Realise either
and will continue to react outside to feelings they're unaware of.
We all inhabit this World & respond in our turn ~ being here now

1

<u>Partial List of Mental Illnesses</u> <u>(Wikipedia)</u>
Acute stress disorder, Adjustment disorder, Agoraphobia, alcohol and substance abuse, alcohol & substance dependence, Amnesia, Anxiety disorder, Anorexia nervosa, Antisocial personality disorder, Asperger syndrome, Attention deficit hyperactivity disorder, Autism, Autophagia, Avoidant personality disorder, Bereavement, Bibliomania, Binge eating disorder, Bipolar disorder, Body dysmorphic disorder, Borderline personality disorder, Brief psychotic disorder, Bulimia nervosa, Childhood disintegrative disorder, Circadian rhythm sleep disorder, Conduct disorder, Conversion disorder, Cyclothymia, Delirium, Delusional disorder, Dementia, Dependent personality disorder, Depersonalization disorder, Depression, Disorder of written expression, Dissociative fugue, Dissociative identity disorder, Down syndrome, Drapetomania, Dyspareunia, Dysthymic disorder, Erotomania, Encopresis, Enuresis, Exhibitionism, Expressive language disorder, Factitious disorder, Female & male orgasmic disorders, Female sexual arousal disorder, Fetishism, Folie à deux, Frotteurism, Ganser syndrome, Gender identity disorder, Generalized anxiety disorder, General adaptation syndrome, Histrionic personality disorder, Hyperactivity disorder, Primary hypersomnia, Hypoactive sexual desire disorder Hypochondriasis, Hyperkinetic syndrome, Hysteria, Intermittent explosive disorder, Joubert syndrome, Kleptomania, Mania, Male erectile disorder, Munchausen syndrome, Mathematics disorder, Narcissistic personality disorder, Narcolepsy, Nightmares, Obsessive-compulsive disorder, Obsessive-compulsive personality disorder, Oneirophrenia, Oppositional defiant disorder, Pain disorder, Panic attacks, Panic disorder, Paraphilias, Paranoid personality disorder, Parasomnia, Pathological gambling, Paedophilia, Perfectionism, Pervasive Developmental disorder, Pica, Postpartum Depression, Post-traumatic stress disorder, Premature ejaculation, Primary insomnia, Psychotic disorder, Pyromania, Reading disorder, Reactive attachment disorder, Retts disorder, Rumination disorder, Schizoaffective disorder, Schizoid, Schizophrenia, Schizotypal personality disorder exist in the auras in y/our fields of energy. We are all susceptible, to life ~ Allowance of the Experiences in your Chi

Yogesvara ~ Master of all the Mystic Power
Recognisance, Renaissance, Transcendence of 'Reality'
Isn't it true Ancient knowledge was based on this Sub-Atomic,
Quantum, holistic, fractal, genetic sub/Conscious Realisation?
Taught in many environments ~ 'The Bhagavad Gita' is famous,
"O lotus eyed Krishna is 'The Cause of All Causes'
The Source of All Illumination".
Shows his Transcendental * Universal eternal formula,
entering into his Material Manifestation to teach Arjuna.
"Every living Entity is only a Spiritual Spark" Not 'disorder.'
It's Impossible to understand by mind this Unlimited Infinity.
Discerning Material Form and all pervasive Spiritual Reality.
Revelation is not possible for those of Mental Speculation
but meeting through devotional service, not being attached
to a Tourettes' glitch the 'disability de jour' tickling your box!
Syndromes, chronic disorders, out of Sense perceptions.
"I give you divine eyes to see my mystic opulence."
Seeing the All Expanding, Unlimited Universal form
(BG ch. 11.13) not with Mind but Spiritual eyes ~
to see, don't change your Mind, change your vision
as if 100,000 inexhaustible Suns arose at once.
Blazing radiance in the sky * heating the Universe…
Sitting in a Chariot with Krishna observing the Wondrous

*

Playmates of Krishna
Attracted by loving features not displays of wealth.
Immersed in pure Love ~
Immeasurable like the Sun
Brahma sitting on the Lotus flower
Shiva playing with his divine snakes
Unlimited the Origin ~ no end or beginning.
(BG ch. 11. 25-32) 'The law of nature is non attachment'
(BG ch. 2. 11) "Knowledge is to know Matter & Spirit ~
And the controller of both"

3

It's All Existence.
Four million assembled on the Kurushektra Battlefield;
10 survivors! & what about HIV in Africa or India today?
TB, polio, trauma flashbacks from Class-room attacks,
and living as a blind person how do you see any light?
Their own body is 'Immaterial' they can't see 'disorders'.
Feeling the essence shining inside with golden radiance.
*What about recidivists, many types of diagnosis, **let it go** ~*
"Never was there a time when I did not exist; there is no you
nor all these kings, nor in the future shall any of us cease...
to be Alive in the heart of every living entity" (BG.ch. 2.12).
"All are eternally Individual beings both in Liberation and
conditioned situations", always in existence so don't lament.
The supreme is separated by the cover of Illusionary Maya.
Awareness is merging into Brahma's impersonal, infinite aura
of continuous immateriality ~ Impermanent Buddha vibrations.
Take your pick once through the veil ~ (a metaphor for sacred).
Being liberated from diagnosis, separated Conditioned States.
Self-realised not being upset by changes of a body or 'disorders'.
It finally transmutes ~ the body itself (life's relative imperfections).
"Rejoice at the rejuvenating of this living energy" ~ Are you ready
for the more superior enjoyments of this material existence?
Physical & mental phenomena are human definitions. 'Quantum'
*is intrinsically transcending all the **'disorders'** and imperfections.*
Always changing, non-permanent; death is the end coming from
***Sense Perceptions** ~ tolerate them without being disturbed.*
(BG ch. 2.15) "Liberation is Not upset by happiness or distress"
I know words are very easy compared to the 'Reality of Pain!'
Being 'Cosmic*boundlessness' ~ 'Spiritual is Impermanence'
Mind/body is permanently changing ~ that's Nirvana brother!
"Changing Matter ~ Spirit is Eternal, Knowing the difference."
Being Self Illuminated * Spiritually existent back in your semi!
Removing this dual Ignorance of Spirit & Matter (BG ch.17)
"That which pervades the body is Indestructible"

It's Always Changing

Climate change is a blip for Mother Earth but be Aware ~
(BG ch. 2.17) 'Consciousness is spread all over the body'
Conscious of pains & pleasures ~ of the body/mind's limits.
"Don't know how you feel darling but it was great for me!"
Only this Material body is destructible, embodied beingness,
we all will die somewhere under a sub atomic, starry lit sky.
"Never commit Violence to anyone, it is abominable"
'Arjuna's engaged in killing for Religion' It's hard to accept!
'A thrill to wind you up' Source of energy from the Heart.
You are engrossed in ontological anxiety, moroseness.
Captivated as the enjoyer of the fruits of the mind's tree ~ Eve.
The Material body, I like to enjoy the life, witnessing its reality.
I'm not a monk and need to experience full human happiness ~
Enjoying Osho's insight & wit in this Mirage Controlled Reality'
coerced in us by masters of political power & fundamentalists.
Have to have time to relax, chill out, travel, enjoy her kisses ~
still witnessing (not forgetfulness) streams of consciousness.
What do you Believe? Embrace a divine doctrine of devotion;
Loving Kindness & Compassion taking you to transcendence.
Find the Unmanifest, No Form* Space before or after human life,
but you have to be detached from any Identity, any Programming.
However wonderful it may seem, remember it's all a deep dream.
Be the Cosmic witness and enjoy full Psy*trancing in Anjuna.
Feel the butterfly flying freely in the clear blue summer sky.
I say enjoy a smile from your heart & from her soft lips.
Importance to be able to flow above the Mind, being kind.
Remember lying in your arms, 'I Am'*'AS IT IS' Spiritually.
Opening for us the doors to Heavenly Planets * Galaxies.
To do your duty without Expectation Arjuna; everything is done
for Transcendental Consciousness, the highest quality of Action,
of being, so No Reaction from Mental Activities, just Surrendering.
No longer attached to sense gratification, definitions of joy or illness.
Realising the distinction between Spirit & matter * simply beingness

The Greatest Warrior Commanding Elephants
Seeing you in wonder off the battlefield
All perfected ~ your body is Immaterial.
Sitting, feeling Kundalini ~ lava rising in your Yoni
and Individual Star crossed lovers of eternal entity.
Kama Sutra Yoga free from bondage, being bliss ~
Living without the fruit of a throbbing Karmic tree.
'Samadhi', from the Vedic dictionary, 'A Fixed Mind'
When the Mind is fixed for Understanding the Self.
It's not possible for those captivated by the senses,
condemned by the processes, of Material Energies.
Be free from all dualities, from any gainful anxieties;
Be established in the self (yoga). Have no guilt feelings,
pain & fear because you're Attached to the Sensations!
Lovely reading the poetry of Vyasadeva, dancing at dusk
Om a Starlit beach

*

Lila Pastime
'Her disorders are only sense perceptions'.
Met her in a State of cosmic trance ~
In ecstatic dance * flux of hot Romance.
Don't grieve for the destructible body by knowing,
Inconceivable, immutable, Invisible, all pervading
eternal energy ~
Always existing, undying, primeval
free by witnessing, not forgetfulness
swimming in streams of consciousness
She is spread all over you ~
Changing in front of your eyes.
& Inside of you.
We'll change and meet in another body ~
I'll kiss pure spirit on your smooth moist lips.
In another destiny we'll mix our energy
Eternally you & me ~ forever free

'Saumya ~ Vapuh' Sanskrit: The Most Beautiful Form
Surrender Your Self, Your Mind, Your thinking Ego ~
Use your Mind and body to do this especially when down.
When the ego is weak, at the rock bottom, in a mess, zero,
lost with no hope. Surrendering becoming Humble, for once
in your life. Use this Experience to let Mind's 'disorders' ~ go.
This is a Unique special moment although you're too busy in
Suffering to see it, to go beyond any Pain. It doesn't have to
be a full, complete tragedy. This is the silver lining, it takes you
through the Gates of hell ~ Like Arjuna not wanting to fight a War;
Krishna told him.
"The wise lament neither for the living nor the dead" (BG ch.11).
"Knowing the Unknowable, Absolute Truth from a surrendered soul"
Time for 'Reconditioning' You see Krishna through
Spiritual ~ the non material eyes of Revelation
*

The Interaction of Energies
Krishna ~ 'the Cause of All Causes'
Ordinary people came to know why he appeared
on Earth and executed such Wonderful, Amazing acts.
Coming to know 'bhakti' 'devotion' Spiritual*Consciousness.
Relieving a person from all problems, their 'disorders' of Life.
If a Man is Suffering it's due to his Forgetfulness of his Eternal
Relationship to Krishna Spiritual Consciousness
Relationship ~ Activities but don't be Attached to the Result.
Do it with Spiritual Consciousness of the boundless space.
Birth and death are limited to Material, mind/body worlds ~
(nama/rupa), not spiritual awareness or Krishna consciousness.
Frequencies, densities, gravities, less worry, less anxiety.
"Fear is due to one's absorption in Illusory energy"
"The human body is meant for spiritual Realisation"
(BG. pp. 171/2) Brahma is the Original creature ~
Hearts & souls submerging at the lotus feet of Krishna

Supernatural * Omniscience
Releasing the Brain ~ Indefinitely
Being here now is * Infinitely*Infinity ~
Learning to detach from this World Form.
A process of elimination & witnessing.
And what is the use of words?

*

Razzle Dazzle
The Mind Screams
"I hate you > always!"
Tell the Mind to Love her.
Mind got the Order
Eliminate the Word
Tuning ~ (with her)
beyond No-mind, Space
Inevitable

*

Razzia's Dispassion
Can there ever be too much compassion?
Weaken the leash (drop the shields),
conflict in the Inner being.
True energy fields ~
Kissing electromagnetic juicy peaches
on a Priestess of Venus' ripe wet lips.
Diving to the depths
up to the surface.
In the end
You gotta go through it alone ~
No teacher, no master; found your Inner guru.
"Stolen from Africa brought to America"
Even voted them back in, the Warmongers!
I'm dealing with my reality, the best I can
my friend…
Inner beauty

Karmaless Krishna

To know the Eternal Spiritual life, free from Materialism ~
Free of Mental Speculation, friendly to each living entity..
The source & All Pervading energy, Master of all Mystery
Free from being selfishly attached. (BG. Ch.18. pp. 51-53).
'One always in trance is detached & free from false Ego'

*

On the Krishnaloka Planet in the Spiritual Sky

To Know What Is Spirit & What Is Matter! "One should not spend
one's time pondering over how to make money". (BG) 'Brahma-
Bhuta' ~ Oneness with the Absolute Transcendental Krishna
Consciousness. Elevated to Self-Realisation helps you put the
Human Condition, our reality, Y/our 'disorders', y/our fears,
y/our neighbour's Suffering, their Anxiety causing ~
distressful frequencies of disease into the Full Context.
Pure Devotion, no negativity, 'Bhakti' is a State of Liberation.
What to do with your crazy son? Real illusory attachments ~
of a mother & father, while words are relatively easy to give.

*

'Night Watch' - A Russian Horror Film!

"Are the Ingredients Important or the Effect?"
"The World hasn't changed, just You"

*

Spiritual Eyes

Seeing Krishna in Your Heart, with a clear Mind at Peace.
By Love and devotion can't see anything else. (BG ch.11).
"Reached the Supreme Planet after leaving the body"
Be transcended ~ become Perfect while doing your work.
Anything done for Personal Sense Gratification is a Cause
of Bondage ~ but I love my daughter's birthday too And
Celebrating at Goa trance parties with beautiful Russian
dancers, juggling fire sticks on a full moon beach ~ 'Dada'
Have to let the dogma go too and be cool with yourself.
Realising Space to live in peace with purring Radharani

9

Ambient Radiation ~ in the air we breathe invisibly.
Man Made fields Electronically ~ Wi-Fi. flowing digitally
"You can convert to any religion, doesn't bring you closer to God"
"It's easier to apologise than ask for Permission."
Just go and do it again; dishonest Corruption!
Not to be a slave; Programs of the Sun ~
*There goes my little flower * win win situation.*

*

Transmutating ~Turn that energy in the right direction
by getting detached from the wrong direction, thing!
Love is only for the Divine being forever ~ changing.
Nobody's desires are fulfilled, so you want a rebirth.
Trapped by your own free-will, it's called MAYA.
She is the Goddess' energy of all your Illusions ~
and desires, impossible to resist her in your mind.
Maya doesn't disturb the meditation of Shiva ~
Although she's always trying to get his attention

*

M O M E N T
"It's not a dog or a cat it's a soul!"
Accept, step out of the conditioning
Don't be with demons be with the present
not the consequences coming to haunt you.
You should have no goals you are it, let the I AM go too.
Tricks you into believing you are it, I AM; IT'S NOT YOU!
I am everything going beyond your mind's Form of identity,
beyond the Universal manifestation into dark matter ~
Shakti, Parvati, she runs the world, she's the energy
Beyond that experienced as mother nature….
Beyond that of the intellect and rational brain.
You wanna follow your blind faith?
Temptations like the Devil.

<u>Accepting Our Beingness Not a Computer Programmed Neocortex</u>
Is there any reason so many of us go out of our Minds ~
in the wrong way without knowing why, and how we can
once there, deprogrammed, explore the Spiritual Cosmos
instead of dying with Addictions, obsessions, guilty DNA;
stress disorders no one knew the names of or their existence!
Yet many go through life with sad strife, or as his mad wife
who never knew she had 'Reactive Attachment disorder' ~
No blame or shame, being lost in this judging, diagnosis game.
(see Disorder lists & levels of consciousness on pages 52-53)
Your 'Borderline Personality disorder' friend & your ADHD fun!
Making us react to abuse; expectation wants the perfect son.
Your 'crimes' are not seen as 'Passive Aggressive behaviour' or
even 'Oppositional Defiant disorder'; needs more than defiance or
Zero tolerance, needs psy*trance dancing to transcend these perceptions.
How to ascend, align with these Mental-objects-movements; to consciously
get a glimpse of Mr. Buddha's friends & Miss. Radha's Quantum hologram?
How to respond freely with your mum's cancer, to hold her hand, to just be ~
connecting through our 3rd eye ~ witnessing, being the observer of your ego,
of our 'Apparent Reality', of all segregated material manifestations, identities ~
Creating an image for our contaminations until we Realise our divine essence
Keep your Mantra alive ~ You are Not this Form in Streams of Consciousness.

*

Your seeds of life ~ keep growing up into the Spiritual sky
Pervading in the heart of every atom to re-establish their
relationship with Spiritual world. **Recognising** synchronicity
in Schizophreniform disorder, Seasonal affective disorder,
Self Injury, Separation anxiety disorder, Sexual Sadism
& Masochism, Shared psychotic disorder, Sleep disorder,
Sleep terror disorder, Sleepwalking disorder, Social phobia,
Somatization disorder, Specific phobias, Suicide Stereotypic
movement disorder, Stuttering, Tourette syndrome, Transient
tic disorder, Transvestic Fetishism, Trichotilomania, Vaginism.
Transcending interpretations, mind, fears, enjoy being here now.

I've never had it this bad Crusher
Absolutely has to be a threat for Love to Conquer All...
"They Fucked me in the Mind!" Get yourself a New Robot.
You are bigger than this, seeing it in a Relativity context ~
Practical, look for a Positive in a Negative ~ it's all impermanence."
Re-establishing their Spiritual World of changing*transcendence!
Inheriting a 'neurological disorder' at the onset of childhood from
genetic, environmental factors but the exact causes are unknown.
Not a good medical prognosis unless a bodhisattva tells you it's illusion!
It came on a caravan with a bunch of miming Coprolalians in dreamtime.
Arriving on the battlefield at Kurukshetra for an amazing Spiritual lesson.

*

Welcome Shiva*Destroyer of the Material Universe.
I've surrendered to a daughter of Brahma Kumara ~
Another tended devotedly to Krishna's cows at Surabhi
'Rasa' * in your face, reflections of a lovely sunbeam ~
Her true Love fell from radiant sparkling stars of the Supreme.
The last words of the Buddha, "everything is impermanent, work
out your own salvation with diligence" seek no refuge but yourself,
your inner guru; Krishna & Buddha's blessings shared with everyone.
Teachings of Transcendence ~ through Bhakti, devotional service,
Loving Kindness & Compassion. 'Bodhisattvas would rather allow
themselves to be killed than to kill, to keep the peace and right karma ~
knowing this body is an illusory FORM of your Mind's (dis/orders) reactions.
King Asoka did his duty and realized after witnessing his destructive powers
that it's essential to know the difference between material & spiritual states.
Sitting under a sacred Peepal tree in Meditation, freaking out in a War Chariot
or kissing long, puffy nipples at the Temple of Venus in tantric contemplation?
The giant egos of a Darius, Caesar, Alexander, Ramses, warring catalysts!
Why accept, who needs them? What's the definition of a cult of Sociopaths?
From the Stoners Age to Now ~ hologram, quantum, nano, zero-point galaxy
"I've lost All My Power!" "Freeing up the Mind!" Processing human delusions.
Before coming onto the battlefield ~ Cosmic Alchemysticism

Living Life
People think they have to Judge ~
Interpret, identify, react to, do or die!
Stopping it all by feeling inner Peace.
Peace Is In You
A Transcendence ~ of Form.
We react to the Object of the Mind.
The Subject is its live essence
If it wasn't that nothing would be.
The dream is the happening
the plane of reality allowing Consciousness.
You gotta deal with yourself * wherever you go.
WAKE UP!

*

In the Zone
"I don't believe in Aliens; what the fuck's just happened?"
There's something going on here, that's OBVIOUS now!
They have hidden stuff, corrupt accounts all over the World.
Prime Minister it's all heading in paranoid directions, correct?
Swept through a Vortex of emotion that I couldn't control ~
Thinking about something wrong, I had to get to the bottom
of before I worked it out. That's where we all end up, fucked!
A thought is such a simple thing, then you realize, understand
this fantastic thing that we are is not what you imagined it to be

*

Inflexible * Full of Vanity
"Open your legs like a butterfly,
put the ignition key in ~ "
Innocence live from the Heart
Blazing in their Cosmic Kisses.
"Judge us not for our weakness but for our Love"
Kashmiri Space ~ Is this Paradise?

Qu'est ce que c'est?

You don't want to watch movies about Psycho-women.
"Sexually frustrated wankers are scared of hysterical women!"
'By 2050 there'll be more plastic in the sea than fish!'
Quantum Reality * blinking in and out of existence
In every moment
We can cease to manifest it at all
It's an hallucination but it feels real.
Ants won't cross a line of cinnamon.

*

Owning your own deeds of Chaos & Cause

Always making it ~ now, touching out to Neptune.
Sowing and reaping in Synchro*Parallel Universes.
A long distance for morality, evil & Love to travel ~
Just being here & there in your Merkaba Spaceship.
Light years from a previous condition that came into
Existence in your Mind

*

Ahimsa for Sociopaths

'No one will come out of a Nuclear war alive!'
Ask Shiva, what the fuck happened at Fukushima!
These are the Corporate Governments of the Apocalypse!
Poisoning, irradiating, traumatizing, alienating, murdering
Our Planet, our Mother Nature and our Children's future ~
We sit on our hands and whine about the idiot in the Palace.
Get a fuckin grip people!

*

Ponds Need Feeding

Make an Indian girl Miss Universe creating a new product, market
for the Corporates to enter and sell her essential whitening cream!
Being manipulated through Maya, selling us images of beauty humans crave.
Taught us, brainwashed, diverting our attention to the next crisis, abyss, terrorist!
False news, pseudo intellectuals working for the Matrix, controlling y/our thoughts.
No Heart, No Feeling ~ only has a hungry pussy!

Kali Alaikum

*Bring it on full power giving our energy to the Governor
of fear; she brings you beyond Time ~ ½ Shakti * ½ Shiva.
Male & female, containing every energy; Divine Mother, Ma.
I love that little sexy phone; 'a brighter side of Neptune' "Salam"
Stay in eternity everything is Meditation ~ witnessing it all change.
Flowers of life, no need to force, by the Grace of God, Revolving
Inside the macroscope*inside the microscope ~ Spiralling heart's
Cosmic milky ways of expanding love.
Arriving at an island, spent the weekend with a proper wallah.
Life is sweet, jumping into a cenote of Love, working with violet
flame channels (not throwers), in lands of the dove. Visions from
above ~ In a spaceship with Indigo children. Allowance to unfold
eternal moments ~ transmitting vibrations, transmuting reflecting
frequencies ~ Now the mirror's getting very strong ~ into beingness.
Earth's heart chakra makes the circle round * multi-dimensional
beings in human form, at the poles ~ the Earth goes inside itself.
Psychic Cyber AI. war on many dimensions, love friction ascending to
higher revolutions * LSD * Certainly I don't need a plasma HD. 3D. TV.
Like fire moths*all drugs changing ~ of a culture; football fans pilled up in
ecstasy ending the mindless, ugly violence, brawling on the tribal terraces.
Mad drunken aggression, cocaine & amphetamine made it extreme again!
Psychedelic chilling out on tropical beaches ~ blissful in Aphrodite's arms.
Who's going against Nature's grain, chaos within the heart of a hurricane?
Sai Baba calling in dreams; showing me streams of consciousness to swim,
deep channels to surf ~ Falling into the Pools of Love's Imprint. Reflexions ~
Spirit shining in this energy, awakening, freedom burning, Inspirational lives,
evolving, regardless of ego-mentalist, dramatic ~ Object Time-Space bombs!
Who is nurturing Mother Earth? We're here interacting as the biggest Blessing.*

"You have to Love yourself to be able to Love others"
And to be Free in the Love ~
'Relating truly in the moment'

*Natural relationships ~ everyone shares, not being a Slave!
Who has to pay for joy? You/we/me make y/our own Realities*

At the Bad Boy Bar

Each moment ~ comes out of the boundlessness as your creation.
Realise multi energetic dimensions * everything will be fine because
there's No judgment, no more fake material, ego frame for the flame.
A Magician's own reality, electromagnetism changing Planetary
polarity, giving juice to Mother Earth. Overpopulation or less ~
It's all in the heart but it's always passing through the dual Mind
You're Mindful * Mindless ~ Observe its changing as a Witness!
We are only energy cells, nothing gets lost; being omnipresent.
Manipulations of Mass/Time & Space crossing on the tides ~
don't wait for no wo/man, no race, simply relax in omniscience.
That Mind Set ~ about the Planet, your breath, Om your path.

*

Dionysus on Dialysis

Deep brain stimulation; Monitoring, someone covertly watching!
"What do I know, What does s/he know, What do they know?"
Ad Infinitum ~ NOW we understand what you're doing NWO!
I'm home ~ where you are, where you can be Yourself.
Not many Train spotters on platforms collecting numbers
Monkey with a Mind, Conquering Monkey; #1 Awareness
of the Consequences! A chemical Reaction Conscience ~
Whose 'Visions of the Liquid Earth'? Bottom line living
with yourself ~ as soon as you think you understand it
You're Lost! If people only admitted they didn't know
or have a clue! "I'd be the first to do that." Natural Lips.
No numbers, Cosmic Petals, Free Spirits*Infinity Airways.
A Good Mantra, Why Not, Why > definitely on the bridge.
Cosmic Cruiser's floating, it's everywhere ^ have a laugh.
Making black Kali Chillums; progression not another Test.
No Judgment>the Old Programming ~'gently down the stream'
Dreaming not screaming, guard my heart when a lover goes ~
"I wouldn't come here if it wasn't Insane, I wanted to get lost."
Lose 20 kg. become a thin, insomniac speed freak; No thanks!

Trans*Fusion

Carlos Castaneda was an Anthropologist but also
a Conceptual Artist flying on surreal cactus fuel.
I am not a poet painter essentially I'm a Creative Artist ~
Not being Scientific, not making sense, being Abstraction.
Manifesting Surreal, expressive and perceptional Intention.
Came across an ethnopoet from the Huichol of Oaxaca.
carrying a bunch of radiant psychotropic 'Power Plants.'
He got a doctor's degree for his 'Teachings of Don Juan'
'A Separate Reality' & 'Journey to Ixtlan'
"God is everywhere and in everything"
Met a Yacqui Shaman at a bus stop in Nogales, New Mexico.
Spiritual rhythms, symmetry, fractal patterns of synchronicity ~
The Blue scout in a blue mosque, pure light, pure Cosmos
Visual Landscapes of Beautiful Nature, Divine Being ~
Spontaneous marks reflecting Inner unity from Chaos
'Psychic strings to Universal sympathies
getting in touch deep within ourselves'
*
*

You have to Inhale

Taking shamanism seriously, into hidden mystic worlds.
Plants have a spirit, they can teach us what they know.
Took Peyote, flew as an owl into the Emerald Cactus
Met an ancestor of the ether, scared out his Mind ~
turning into a howling, iridescent black dog.
Met a native, took the 'Intention Training'
All the Universe is going on in his Mind
Observing being an expanding Participant
Skill of divination * hallucinatory visionary Sorcerer.
On a journey to the Pass of Mental collapse.
Biology breaking down his defences, his Identity,
his self conscious conditioning, his world view ~
different Insights ~ realities between dimensions
to save his sanity

Predators Lost in Irony
Anyone Remember Check Point Charlie, the Bay of Pigs?
Halle Berry for La Presidente of a Paranoiac Tinsel Town!
"We're cranking out Missiles like sausages", Khrushchev.
'Outspending them on Bombs - to Stop The War!'
'Strategy of the Great Game' do you see the Irony?
Capped him, "You only pull out a weapon to use it"
Amazing to envisage it's all just frequencies ~
'You got three cherries in a Row'
Bar Bar Bar
_7   7   7_
We'll believe until the last instant.
_*_

Rocket * Tree
Is there a Key
Is it Locked ~
Why isn't it Open?
Love affair ~ with longevity
nobodies complaining
about 42 years of happiness
NO JEALOUSY
"for me it's just fuckin....
Why Imagine any barrier, any Lock?"
"Bring me the crazy Generals!"
_*_

"Independent but workin' as a brickie, family of 4"
Attached * always attached, Not free to be ~
Let the attachments go, dissolving into detachment...
If you let the Mind go ~ lets the pain go with the Ego.
Detached, non attached, to something holding you.
Then you're in that Zone but keep it Real too!
Outside all the definitions ~ Somewhere.
I'm always going to try to bring it back
to being frequency

18

In a Depression ~ Looking for Lucidity
Safer behind a Virtual Big Wall, Separating Them from Us ~
You're allowed to do this but not that. Not allowed to go here but
you can go there, thank you! Controlling, splitting your whole being,
making a separation between who has water or not, who can work,
who can travel, study, pray, who has life! Right & wrong, up & down,
yesterday & tomorrow, friends & enemies that you've never even met.
Killing them cruelly with your ego for us! Laws, Criminal Justice Bills'
which stop you talking to neighbours & your kids playing in the street!
Is it any wonder we're dysfunctional with a splitting personality,
Afraid & paranoid? Intentions & Motivation of forces giving you
perceptions of Yourself and Reality in which we all must survive!
What happened to 'Les Droits Humains' with Crimes Against Us,
Humanity? Your Medical Records are being scrutinised, you can
be sectioned, your private self is usurped. You lost your sense of
your own true Identity. Had a break down, naturally got AA for my
Brain disorder. ADHD; Short term memory loss led into Dementia.
When you left I went Insane affecting my behaviour, emotionally, my
nerves, brain; don't know any more. Putting the pieces back together.
Woke up in nightmares sometimes had panic attacks. How much do
I allow myself, how do I understand My*self & You in this landscape?
Obsessions, Addictions, Cravings, Fear, Madness all around;
Insecurities, they're all dimensions of 'suffering' to a Buddhist.
What's the answer? Look at all these 'disorders' accepting the
World is a dangerous place, having to develop Consciousness
to put it into true perspective, to let it go into the spiritual realm,
happily on its way ~
*

No Expectations, Liberated & Enlightened
From the Patterns * grounding us in this 'Reality'
Non-Transcendence; Live ~ being the 1000 petalled Lotus.
What's the modern definition of a Militarised Police State?
These 'disorders' put into context ~ of 'Zero Tolerance'
We've lost the Quatrain ~ 'On Heavenly * Mountain'

<u>Blame Supplements</u>
Need to boost your Serotonin levels, try 5-HTP herbals!
Friend Van Gogh, **Bi polar** 'disorder' exorcised in his painting.
"al-Qa'ida deserving death more than you desire life." Nutters!
"Use the Drone!" Confirming our 'Intelligence'... Where's it at?
Washington bound, 'No Due Process' An Enemy in the house!
The World is Paying the Price of these Maniacs & Usurpers;
Their Cluster bombs are Indiscriminate, Legal Collateral Evil!
Criminals presenting Psy-Ops, lies; 'Yellow Cakes' to Congress.
Put it in his 'State of the Union' address, 'Uranium from Africa!'
UK intelligence, Co conspirators spreading untruths, Iraq to Niger.
*

Paradise is what you make it
What's wrong with that Judge?
Hopefully I just broke that 'Virtual Mould'
Who I was for Who I am, just havin' a go ~
I've always been following a twinkling Star from afar.
Never giving up all my freedom to give you only pleasure.
Inscription of a Traveller, being happy, always changing.
All waves coming together simultaneously, so loved up!
Creativity becomes more fulfilling ~ complete.
Freeing yourself from the chains of a Master!
Free Inside ~ Outside the Concepts of a Mind.
FINDING YOUR INNER GURU
* Embracing the Universe *
Took me there showing me the possibilities.
This is what I do...
We're here, nothing better, than now ~
Clean, clear and fresh, the total inside line.
No discrimination; I'm in Love with a woman,
rings through her nose & lips. The real ones.
Right here in my head banging away.
Let the Love Talk

'Freedom's just another word for nothing left of Ego'
"UK's. DNA. Database has 3.7 million samples; 6% Pop.
More than One million taken from people Never, ever
convicted of an offence (20.01.07 Independent, London).
The 1ˢᵗ from 1995; now this is shared with multi-national
databases. All new born babies from 2007 to be included.
The World's most ambitious Identity scheme!" Thank You!
Need to Relax our Privacy laws, gauging the public reaction.
Central metadata; each movement Filed In their Perfect field.
Hiding in the mountains ~ go there first and make Shanti Om.
*

Bioneers*Palliative
'There is some nudity ~
Hospitality as a sacred duty...
She took him straight to Paradise
*

Lava lamp
The Mind can't do it >I don't know < What Mind Is?
Clean and Clear ~ we know intuitively, what's right
& wrong. Truth as a basis of reality * Synchronicity..
Tao rattling on with the monkey ~ Feel it, Keep it Real.
Shiva's India embracing the Universe, no more Time ~
Met a Spacewoman who likes being chatted up, why not?
A golden horizon; Sky giving them 'Reality' on Satellite TV.
Opium eaters, spent 17 years in a Banyan tree, observing ~
Fields of Marigolds & Strawberry forests seemingly forever.
I've given up on it ~ helps, floating in seas of no stressfulness.
Xtending it until Swept overboard.....
*

Pure Expressionism
Pretty chilled, Jim wanted them all to go through the Doors.
Together we could all be sexy angels, being high in the sky.
"We've all got a Jackson Pollock hiding in us somewhere mate"
Let them know we'll go! Not scared of a fight to get the honey.

<u>Darkness & Light</u>
**'You can only get rid of Unconsciousness
by Consciousness, not a poisoned heart!'**
*Asleep you've got to wake up ~
Generated by illusions of the mind.
Problems from the past, in the future ~
memories, Imagination running wild!
What about being here now!
Not caught up in the head
causing pain. If you know
then just project happiness.
Inspiration's deep Inner Space*

*

<u>Very deep and beautiful</u>
*… and one day he wanted to fuck off to Paradise!
"The greatest thing you'll ever learn is
just to love and be loved in return."
'Transcending through the heart the part
of man connecting with woman'
The village gave him a young wife
the first day he got there ~*
**Most people ate the cake.
Yeah everyone!**

*

<u>Lust Bulbs!</u>
**"They got you by the Heart*chakra
they can turn that into a black hole!"**
*Your own Mind is controlling, it's all made in You.
You can't help it ~ in Kali's Space it's full of Maya.
Enjoying life as a human ~ that's happening naturally.*
A SLAVE TO MY SENSES or not *~ Chillum central!
Running after Sensual desires just satisfying your own Ego!
Tantric Gurus retiring to Shambala with their sexy Queens.*

A pink candy striped skittle
"With a woman called Fushia and her daughter Cerise, leaving
a club called Spots (in Leicester), were attacked by N F. yobs!
Helped by a Pakistani Taxi driver.....
pushed by a drunken bum in the street.
She was standing next to a bobby
in a doorway on his walkie-talkie."
*

Allowing free expression
Seriously ~ "Suggesting colour equivalents of Cubism"
Releasing your sentiments from Natural Catastrophes...
Bondage, Pain, suffering, crazy losses brawling with ignorance.
Reconfiguring yourself to be liberated ~ from the Attachments.
Playing without thoughts ~ naked carnival dancers in ecstasy
*

Punk Protection
She Stepped outside the Frame of reference into no-man's land.
He was a nano-Robot with Asperger's; elemental and relentless!
Living in the UK where 90% of heroin on the street comes from
Helmand Province, Afghanistan. Opium production, with mobile-labs
Increased in 2007 by 1/3rd in only one year! How is this possible?
7,000 British troops have been fighting there for five years!
*

*Kali * Maya can drive anyone mad*
I got a Text from England
Daffodils blooming ~
Blackbirds are laying eggs....
Longer days and Golden Sunsets.
Find the primordial Space
Allowing the Form to be
You are the Action ~
Free whirling helping them go on their journey
Everything is Simple ~ natural
As a Rock*Is God

Hot Geranium
What's the carbon footprint of a Tank?
400 tonnes of depleted uranium bullets and shells!!!!!
Fragments exploding in the air poisoning everything alive!
Abandoned days making a lot of new, holy shit crucifictions!
Not for the man who escaped from a straight-jacket ~
*by balancing on his head * the cherry pie was empty!*
What about the pheromone attractions?
"I pissed on a jellyfish!"

*

Idol
"I am Idle!"
"How many Idols can you look at?"
Make me your God and I'll make you my Queen.
Worshipping anything; a guy nailed to a piece of wood!
"It's no good being offered loads of money
If you're not alive to spend it!"
Where's the burnt offering mate?
Need something for a sacrifice to God!
Is this the Divine?

*

Cycles of Unconsciousness
Pleasure is your inner nature ~
Having the wrong ideas because of the Mind & its five senses.
Its function is to keep you from realizing the Divine pleasure!
Keeping you trapped in your desires until you die ~ then rebirth.
They're kept in the biggest Maya; Money, too little, never enough!
"You want petrol for your car you gotta work for it!"
"Mind's reason for existing is to hook you on something.
You start Loving Your desires.
You could be in Love with your gold tipped new pen!
The Mind will make you swoon; it feels sexy, so good!"

Tropical water source

Sweet frangipani * gorgeous yellow hibiscus flowers.
Solomon Islands selling live Dolphins to Dubai, sheiks!
What is the Design for the holy of holies in this Gulf?
Global Infrastructure & Communication for a Prophet.
Channelling energetic friends ~ Opening closed shells.
Stops you doing things when there is a Curfew brother!
Not nice corruption, local mafia politics, closed societies;
doesn't want to be harassed for being a beauty full heart.
'Salam Alaikum' 'Alaikum Salam' ~ our sister and daughter.

*

Other Bio*options

I don't need the structure but more Creative Space ~
It's already happening, encouraging friends to free paint.
Not to fixate on a 10pm deadline but to tune in & relax.
Take it smooth, dance the energy, feel the harmony ~
Spiritual environment for feeding the heart & Infinite.
Fruit trees, water wells, how will it grow in her arms ~
Flowing
straight into the Ocean

*

What happens in the Monsoon?

Season of Rainbows on Venus
There's large explosions on Mars
Full dancing & singing on Saturn
Exotic Pagan festivals on Gaia Earth
Energy regenerates on Pluto's crystal shores
Creation blooms in Neptune's parallax Moons
Storms are flowing over Uranus' drifting dunes
Jupiter hosts a Star picnic for the Shamans of Sirius
Migrations beginning on the hot planes of Mercury.
My friend who stayed said he loved its beauty ~
Very natural with his Incan Sky Goddess

<u>*"I Can't see why You Would Want to Do Anything Else"*</u>
"No motor Skills" nicely smashed ~
You only have so much of a Floodgate
that can be Opened! A freak show in your street.
'Breathe, observe your mind, let the universe do the rest'
You're the Driver of the Spaceship ~ As funny as Hell!
Sending you to the olive tree, there'll be 72 virgins
waiting for you ~ "What a fuckin' Jihad that was!"

*

<u>*A Taliban Retainer slain by Perseus*</u>
"We were sitting out there in the Gobi desert
thinking we shouldn't Operate it. Use a Proxy!"
She had to keep him on a tight leash that weekend.
Every Conqueror, sociopath puts up their own ideas.
Celebrating blowing up 1,700 year old Buddha statues!
We progress erasing the memory of those before?
Avalon Ballroom's Magic Show on continuously ~
Venus Erotica pushing creative boundaries in Berlin.
"Dialling up anything you can think of in 15 seconds"
Fully fuelled up Predators, switching off Adult Pin Codes

*

<u>*Sirius' Instrument*</u>
"Kali Karma personified for 6 million Jews et al"
Their Shiva lingam is a bullet, bomb, missile!
Yoni is the 5 elements creating the material ~
Space is ether, Shiva is the Spirit, left & right
jogging along beside a string of comets ~
Connecting to the higher self in a hippie house
White Dwarfs on holiday, gone to a secret Planet.
Already very different, disguised as black Apollo with Gopis.
Timeless associations of a Star colony beyond any geometry.
Turned up in a Palace of Surreal, Unreal, Super light clarity.
*Love, dream world of Tantra, intra * dimensional mating ~*
Oh no, she was spiked! Trusting in your mantra; fully Shanti

Where did you learn your 'Detention Techniques'?
Forbidden to have mosquito nets in the Red mosque.
We can't hear the monks chanting only screaming!
They shot him 7 times in the head, 'A Hard Stop'
Used '124 grain' ammunition. Dead to Brain > before
the body could react to hold up his hand & say, "porque?"
What about the 'State Peace and Development Council'
a Genocidal junta in the land of dhamma, like so many?
And the World, UNO. sit on their hands again; Useless!
Models of War ~ Guantanamo Bay to Abu Ghraib Prison.
International Laws all flew out the windows; when they
let General Pinochet walk out of the court a free man!
When Demons are left excused, corruption lives in us

*

My home is in Tuscany
A dreamy house amidst rolling hills & countryside.
Light Assignation in beautiful, atmospheric Firenza.
Nymphs discovered dancing on Etruscan carvings
lying in village pools outside Sienna.
Swans wildly animated by her scent.
"Leave all your troubles behind"
Keep that breath for Planting trees ~
if they cut one down; they won't listen to me.
We are here for a reason; thought I was being Mad.
Keeping the balance, stepping into gorgeous Umbria
A bridge ~ crossing through a renaissance of energies

*

Kama Sutra Yoga
69 Asanas with an Indian Tantric Goddess ~ Rati.
Multi fingered, six armed, dancing Nataraj in full heat.
They're not infinite creations, they're finite Self creations.
Children don't quench his thirst for spirits of the World ~
"Your life is the creation of your Mind" Now Looking out
to the Stars * Polishing his lingam in the naked Sun

27

Streaming Banner on Free Hotmail (4/10/2007 UK)
"We know you'll get around to getting a T.V. license eventually.
We just don't want our Enforcement officers to get to you sooner."
'Easier to pay - Harder to Avoid' 'Click here to get a TV License
And get your name off our visiting list'
Do you people need to put up with vicious, coercive threats any longer?
Pay more taxes to Authority, subliminal control in a Police State Culture?
Or you're already so lost, negative and depressed you don't really care?
This shows they've won your soul!
*

*Rise & Shine * E = MC squared * Firing*
"Stick the baby on your heart. How far from Basic Instincts!"
Multi Dimensional ^ Someone Please help her to her feet!
*Goa ~ *Mind Expansion with or without Psychedelics **
'Recognising Incentives Not Penalties but see the Predators'
"How do you get a fallen bird into bed? Piece of cake"
Not cocktails of 'Class A's. We've all got something of everything.
"If you're happy with yourself you can live that"
*'Bhudevi' Goddess of Nature * Got the Sun in my eyes ~*
Nature is not found at the Ritz Carlton but in this Ocean Pearl
*

Crises, Incidents, Conflict, Troubles-Everything but the Sink
Everyday rip offs, worries, depression of your nerves plus
Bailiffs can now enter your castle and there's a War on ~
Just another regular day for a burnt out brain to deal with.
"In partnership with a World Class Cunt" Don't be too hard!
Stressed Manic; as he left he taught her a Magic spell…
She felt an immense transcendental affection ~
*and prayed to Glorious Saint Atomica*Radianta.*
"God forbid you can speak your Mind here" Uh!
Amazement on the lips of a peaking constellation

"If You go above Rishikesh You see Shiva, for sure!"
Have your films changed people's Minds? In which way?
Hollywood is an Unconscious billboard on a hot dry hill.
'Vivendi, Viacom, Sony, AOL Time Warner, Disney'
Spinning yarn to make a brand, writing jokes, clichés,
screenplays for Banks, Donald Ducks & Corporate sucks.
Don't have a Hedging, Mutual Fund; do you have any Trust left?
'The have it all and the have nothings' What does Buddha have
to say or Jesus or Krishna or Mr. Smith? Anything to do with only
securing National Interests not the People's; are they surprised?
"Nice to talk to the World from the bridge of Utopia"
*

Integrity & Dignity behind Two Way Mirrors
Left Yale, went to Jail for embezzlement; what to do?
Didn't have a clue; Captured our boy & beheaded her.
Al-Quaida proxies destroying the land of the two rivers ~
Protecting Tyrants yet we oppose Personal land Mines!
Dropped 3000 tons of munitions on Baghdad's Town Hall
Rwanda & Darfur; Predators stalking by you in the midst.
The World only looks on in feigned surprise; what to do?
What are local power brokers doing to their own people?
Sitting in their Palaces counting their gold, oil & new slaves.
Coveting their neighbours' resources, possessing the means
to destroy, to destroy, to destroy ~ What's its real worth?
*

Terrorism at the Coliseum
"Now we return to Jihad News with Images of War ~
some of our viewers may find distressing" but most of
our viewers are used to them as they see them every day,
here on their favourite Award winning, Global TV. Station!
"How many must die for Caesar to become Great & Greater?
More desensitised, homicidal spectators of a broad Spectrum.
Who Really Owns the other top Corporations, Conglomerations?
Ultimate Release is in Realisation

"Oh it's good to be Alive!"
Psy*Clops' Illegal, covert, Psy-Ops; Shining Strobe lights ~
On every pigment ~ of colour in barren, earthy Olive fields.
"You had a Different Program that's why you had to go ~
travellin' through densities of a red cubist's likes & dislikes.
Introspection, Insights. Order your 'disorder'. If you break it!
Trust is very hard to find and to put back again, ma cherie.
Your mood swings and behaviour drove me fuckin' Mad!!!
Thankfully I had weeks of Meditation in a silent, empty cell,
knew some real stories of Buddha and the Bhagavad Gita!
Where did you get Your 'Normal Cultural Programming' ~
which Government sponsored educational Establishment?
'Brainwashing' is another reason NOT to define oneself
by Any Label ~ Put it all into a bigger * Cosmic picture.
Don't be caught by any of Your 'neurological disorders'
Don't get Captivated by any Desire; there's a Big list!
Connections, Inter*Relations do you feel Undercurrents,
do you Realise your True-Self from genetics Spiralling
up into a Spiritual Sky not a Materialist Universe dear!
Humanity is changing ~ has a dying body & eternal spirit.
You're separated from your godhead by Maya of Illusion.
A covering, a veil, a mirage, your Ego ~ Self in distress.
All part of it consciousness of the Senses giving you pain.
Your Attachment; Believing it really Exists in body & Mind!
Let that delusion go ~ let your disorders resolve into infinity.
*
The Mix
Ultimately regardless of the Myths, religions we are only
a speck in the infinite universe * The 'Tao butterfly effect'
"Wise wo/men lament neither for the living nor the dead"
Don't get caught in the illusion of ADHD however Real!
How to realise this in your world of suffering & delusion.
Words are easy, this pain is unbearable & the pills help!
Realises finite Material world & infinite Spiritual Cosmos

"You Are Flat Out – Flat out of your Mind!"
Psychedelic's effects on your neuro * transmitters
Relationship ~ 5 – Hydroxytryptamine ~ Serotonin
A hormone produced by the brain used as a chemical
Messenger between brain cells * 'Psilocybin'
Only 50 millionths of a gram needed to start!
*You know that 'Reality' is distorted by LSD *
don't confuse 'hallucinogenics' with 'Reality' here ~ now.
Actions of a Psyche delicious Agent, free from gravity
Beyond My Wildest dreams ~ Sacred flowers, plants
In a Cosmogonic Ayahuasca natural Universe.
Dancing twins with eagle feathers in their hair.

*
*

Inside the Brain of a Quetzalcoatle
Multi dimensional * Hemispheres
Mythical & embryological
Beginnings of esoteric ~ Time
Scientific concepts & Shamanism
Inside DNA; outside the fiery Dragon.
Firing flames of the Ayahuasqueros.
Given a molecule of life ….
Containing genetic information
Is the same for all species.
Everyone came from Brazil.
The best lyricist met her on a beach at the break of dawn ~
Dancing Samba; 'Garota de Ipanema' she goes walking by,
discovering double helixes on her soft pink, wet, sultry lips.
Coded in four letters, animate, essences dissolving a Coup d'
Taken over by the Military not the World of sacred Plants!
Somewhere in the Creation myths of Indigenous peoples,
Life's Cosmic energies ~ divine Perceptions of plumed
Serpents in heat, disintegrating their Solar crystals.
Revelations on the Ladders between Earth & Sky
'Gods come down natural beings go up'

Happiness Monopoly

Like Pigs in shit. Ergot on rye; St. Anthony's fires in Salem.
Government Mafias got you over a barrel of global taxation!
'There should be no more suffering, lay down a heavy burden'
Sad death, Mozart ended up a man buried in a common grave.
Head of Counter Terrorism becoming a Witch finder General.
Guilty by Association, brother in a Red Mosque, flood of blood.
'Assumed guilty before being proven Innocent', lost all credibility!
Why not Tests of fire or water, remember those times preacher?
Radiant denouement please forgive me asking for habeas corpus.
The dignity of servants as human beings in an oppressive, feudal time.
You grow up listening to War every day, hearing hearts breaking, crying.
'Poetry is the Door to Music' & 'ius primus noces', what the fuck was that?

*

Manipulating Shares in Apple Pie & Virtual Hedge Funds!
Performing Americans with Global Elites & Carbon gains.
Class War from above; demanding higher & higher profits!
Aug. 22, Started a Bull Market running through the street.
Commercial Oligarchy living in the city, secured by A Wall.
Booming Management, do anything to keep wages low down!
Living on Peanuts is not a myth of nickel & dime workings.
Wearing a name Tag on your chest, 'No Free Lunches', ok!
No Free Time ~ in return (No time to realize who you are).
Living on a thin Line - of Credit (sub-prime, rising crime).
Supplying & Demanding, what comforts of these Riches?
Laws of Nature, Laws of Economics, Corruption of Greed.
What about the 75% of humanity in this World in dire need?
USA's biggest exporter of Capitalism overseas & UK. no.2!
Who owns the Citibank, who are the Invisible Predators?
Which 'Vested Interests' from the Middle East to China?
Who are 'The Middle Men' with an Abundance of Poor?
Changing Ignorance, Kali Yuga ~ 'In A Perpetual War!'
Reality Cheque; "Is this Paradise?" asked an innocent child.
'Money Makes the World Go Around'. So they say.....

Soul
Keep aiming your Mind
High
*

In the process connecting your Mind with your soul.
Relativity ~ Seeing & Inspiring your World interpretation.
Soul's vehicle for Spirit, personal connection to source ~
"So Hey Ho" falling so high into the Terminus, deep abyss.
I'm goin' in; I'll see you on the other side.
Getting to know you ~ never finished…
*Everything is in our soul * Planetary fields*
*Connected * Intuition is the key not a Zombie.*
Not dependent on drugs, horse tranquilisers for a Buzz!
Glimpsing is not an indulgence
KO ~ heart on Charly Chang
Everybody's Amped
when you put it in four walls!
Dive, dive, dive; Tin hat!
Where's your bunker ~
*

An Atomic Bomb
"There's more to it than meets the eye." Last words of Buddha,
"Impermanent are all compound things, work out your own
salvation (deliverance) with Mindfulness." ~Take Your Pick!
At the House of Commons; full of terminally sick, squawking Parrots!
I'm sharing in rainbow gatherings, sacred memory, loving ceremony
*

Poisoned * Diamonds
Terrain ~ their Reign of Terror…
Humanity discovered the structure of its DNA.
A Revolution ~ Mercury blowing in on the wind.
Everybody's talking 'bout the same, same thing ~
Because there is only one thing ~ Unconditional Love.
Scoring, soaring into the 4th dimension of your heart

Oppression of Respect
Arm the monks ~ "Fight Back!"
Against a Cossack army perpetrating the same conditions
that are existing today under the fascists' gun in Myanmar!
Nothing is sacred to this Junta of cruel despots and Tyrants.
World Political Powers turned blind eyes to their terror rising.
That's how it Flux when they've something we want more!
*

Where does it end? With the Vatican City on Fire!
Blindfolded the Geneva Convention & castrated U N.ocks!
Secret Units' black Room > Evil's Camp Nama. Check GPS.
More Atrocities than Abu Ghraib and Guantanamo Bay together!
Lost all credibility with their Task Force 6-26!
The military's most highly trained counter terrorism unit.
There's No Rules for the Pentagon, No Codes of Conduct.
Those Secret CIA. detention camps around our New World.
Even off-limits to the Red Cross, how inhumane, Mr. Rep!
Now can't throw stones at greenhouses in Burma, Senator.
"I can't even imagine why!" Ask (NY Times 19.3.2006).
Ask 'The Director of Our Human Intelligence Agency'.
Where Special Operations Command works in the dark.
Militants, their most highly trained Killers, "Salam Alaikum"
Called it a 'Conflict' in Iraq, 50,000 locals leaving a month.
Do you remember rebooting your crazed RAM memory?
You just had an 'Invasive Procedure' by the M.I. Complex!
Who made you Paranoid, delusional, gave you Dementia?
Found a Clandestine former Iraqi Torture Chamber,
now a US. Interrogation Cell ~ 'Welcome to America!'
Welcome to 'Extraordinary Rendition', being Proud of
the American Civil Liberties Union making a Freedom of
Information Request. Too little & much too late senator ~
Covert Mind Warfare, Inside My Head, can't be true can it?
Don't take any calls; who makes this policy, fake Democracy?
Resurrected Dracula at the NSA.....

World Nomads at Arraial D'Ajuda
Nature beyond comprehension
Halloween Queen shimmering in emerald green.
Dodging that bullet ~ go with the punches.
Brought that species to extinction.
Plant a seed for Happy Daisy

*

New Marriot in the Artic.
"I'm happy I came but glad to be leaving"
"gotta jet dude"

*

Pride
Full Acid colours at the Palio horserace ~
"They'd send out their famous, beautiful
blonde women to meet visiting dignitaries"
Loving it in Sienna

*

"I'm Fearless, Gorgeous"
That's an Image, that's a myth, a Legend and Cliché!
We came from a different Space, Mothership ~
The Chimps still in trees, left in the disappearing canopy.
Found a Rebel group of Angel fish, we'd arrived too late!
Turned up for a Mojave sunset with dolls from Budapest.
Wind kite surfing ~ under cobalt blue Neptunium Moons

*

A Walkin' Product (hooked on lovely long Pearl legs)
'You need it, without it you don't exist!'
Into branded names. (known 400 of them by the age of 12)
Buy any shit. > On Message < history of Public Relations!
"People could only be Passive Victims or Consumers"
What if it breaks, do you really care, right now?
"Pranic breath transcends human consciousness"
"They'll just have to think I'm daft."
An Ascetic counting his money!

Yeah it was touch & go with him
Shooting into the light, out of the Ego.
Doorway to Heaven, no fear of death
Diversity Flexibility Creativity
Not Same Same but impermanently Same ~ different.
Making another mental construction from the Mind-set.
Who's trying to frighten them, filling them with Anxiety?
Coercing hatred; where could he hide his trepidation?
Compression of movement...
Compassion of light
Life giving breath ~
Focus on your breathing
not on your fear.
*

Body Λ T.420/1
Overcome by fear...
Infinite points of light
Breaking out of its cage
'You are Not your Fears'
Are you... "Concentrated points, pixels of Energy"
"An entire Ocean contained within a drop of water."
'Lost Consciousness of Time' ~ with you darling
'Living through Intensified existential Perception'
"Teaches you how to focus your thoughts,
being aware without thinking of Anything"
*

Overwhelmed Senses
Glittering with the Illusions of Suffering...
Breaking your body ~ free from the light,
to break the light ~ free from Your body.
"When you die the light returns to Cosmic
energy fields that surrounds, pervades it"
"Never forget the light is in our hearts"
Travelling to inner galaxies of Mystical dimensions

Polaris Minger
The Ultimate Doomsday Fish!
Swam into Scottish waters ~ Holy Fuck Lock!
Targeted on Glasgow (UK's 3ʳᵈ largest city).
Nuclear Armament ~ spells D i s a s t e r!
"Whit ye daein ya dobber?"
*

Doing it without thinking about it ~ Evidence-Here I am
"He would say that wouldn't he?" Political hypocrisy!
The Arrogant Establishment devouring each other!
The Wall of Silence was coming down and they're....
Demonising, dehumanising the Protesters for Humanity!
Blue Tooth Invisible information passing through Space
Moving through energy fields outside your frequency ~
*PSY-War Ops. travelling to your brain band * Activating!*
"Shall we dance?" Don't hold your breath ~
Now we can get on with saving the Planet
Whatever happened to the Tigers and Polar Bears et al?
Found pictures on a Box of Frosties, Shell signs & mints.
Found their fossils on the seabed at 100 fathoms, nobody cares;
They were Trigger happy! "Never get out the Boat...
Unless you're going all the way ~ Mother fuckers!
*

*3/12/2007: US Admitted they **knew** Iran had No Nuclear arms!*
Can you believe it? Vampires seeing the cow being Sacrificed!
Using Nuclear Bombs from Tehran to Persepolis to Isfahan;
to Exterminate them All! To Protect US from some D|Evil!
It's your call, we are the Savages In Eden. Forgive US!
Into Your Heart of Darkness, not Lamenting for any dead.
Sub-atomic Quantum entities exploding into nothingness!
Feeling my bride's vibrations in multi*dimensional Space ~
A Perilous journey; Is there any Cosmological explanation?
Made its way into Memories; generations of Akashic records.

37

<u>Married in a White Trousseau</u>
Seeing through your **black** Veils of Ignorance ~
False prophets dictating what is Right or Wrong!
Isn't it Criminal to destroy All Tropical Rainforests…
yet print cash, transmuting it into Green backs for a few.
Finally seeing through the Masks of Coercion and Control.
Isn't it wrong to take away human freedom by greed & fear?
Witnessing the mind in all its differences…

*

<u>Met an Unknown Infra-Red Blind Stick Insect</u>
Into an Alien world, dark zones of invisible Predators.
Deep sea jellyfish prey of a trillion years of dramas.
Emperor Penguins arrival; Southern Lights survival.
Aurora Australis * sub-atomic particles travelling ~
through Outer-space entering Earth's Magnetic fields'
All our Consciousness ties us to the rest of the Universe ~
Waves breaking free of your dimension or not breaking free!
Satisfied with Sensory data that went into deep memory
bacterium absorbed into your nervous system
Searching to release the light from the body ~
Jasmine in the luxurious hair of a fragrant coquette

*

<u>Our lights breaking through the Cosmic walls</u>
Aware or Unaware of Parallel Universes next to you ~
Don't have to live in an Insane world, be your true self.
Responsible for the brains' vital signs of a wave range.
His heart composed of tiny stars, a heartbeat…
A dream of daffodils on the first day of spring
Disappearing into the Infinite expansion ~
In the middle of a dark green, Malachite ocean.
Four suns in a Lemon sky, the water was warm
I'm here, right here, with jet black parrots ~
Perfect weather

Real Ordeal*Feel Ideal
'Harvesting data from Social Networking Sites'
Drowning in the sky, floating in your eye's iris.
Universal Rules, Govern you in time and space
Perhaps he was dead no more Full light ~
Out of this World experiences, like it or not...
Cosmic butterflies Pollinating expectant Orchids.
An Ultimate sense of survival, of attachment of ego.
Contact; It finds you, five elements, an Original point.
Flew across the synchronous Galaxy to be with you anew
Breathe in, breathe out ~ let's try an experience of letting go
*
Dreaming Time
Full Fear
Being dead let it be ~
Implied creativity of a Mind
Let all the horizons disappear
Let all the snakes and delusions dissolve.
Directions aware of a new sensation
Broke the Ocean surface
Powerful currents and gliding Thunderbirds
Holistic hallucinations and firing thunderbolts!
Love Saves * Love Slaves
*
Keeping up her Quota.
The Quality of Life
The Quality of Mind * the Quality of Heart
Those ceasing to be biologically alive.
What would happen to this light?
I don't know, witnessing dark energy.
According to my sources, Your Field ~
Messages from an Advanced Civilisation.
Exploring an Emerald and Violet Thermal.
New Discoveries

Hematite Monitor
Our 'Thought Police' Surveillance programs.
Looking for the Top Job; Inside traitor.
Lost his soul to a lethal Conspirator.
Obviously now the dark came in
took the results, shook his World…
Upside down, put into Perspectives.
Believing in a Nightmare of a dream
of a Nightmare; Came true for him.
Counter Cultures, taking no Notice thank you!
Went back to his Intelligence Roots ~
*Realising this Planet's Nature * Is being Totally destroyed!*
System of Ignorance, greed; Capitalist Exploitation, GMO seed.
Insane Control, Power, look at Iraq, Pre/Post Mad Hussein.
Can we see through it ~ which way to the Holy Grails?
*

Sustaining Sustenance
"One Billion People Live on Less than $2 a day"
90% of World's Resources Exploited by 1% of d'elite!
What's its Reality, how it's maintained, its Consequences.
'This System' - Ask Yourself next time you go for a shit
in a Favela or wash your baby in a putrid, oily slum ~
They don't wanna know; it's Always Your Fault, sister!
The Vast, Cruel Machine Keeps us in our Tight boxes,
OBEYING... 'Learn from it don't Judge it' if you can.
*Need a New Paradigm*dimensional shift, soul brother.*
Went Outside their world, got a quick 'no fault' divorce.
The Machine wants you to believe it's the Only Reality -
Persistent abuse, violence, deceit, torture, drumming fear!
Did you ever hear of the murdering of a cult in Jonestown?
Different way of looking at things ~ Who's had a Delusion?
Dangerous paranoiac ordering 940 suicides in the jungle!
I'd rather spend Time in a naked tribe by Black Rock desert.
Making love with a primal Princess of the sunrise and sunset

<u>Molecular biological singing plants</u>
Separated from the garden by your rational, left sided brain?
Beguiling visions flying from within Primitive creation myths ~
Iconographic displays crossing a Peruvian shaman's heart.
He's for the chop connecting mutating viruses!
Conscious Anacondas playing in starry synthesis.
Pure abstract, pure pleasure, dazzling, crystal clear.

*

<u>Brutish Upper Lip</u>
Traitor's treachery; Tony the Righteous bloody Betrayer!
If you are going to Italy you want to flow; like Olive Oil.
Wrong time wrong place, alright I promise within reason.
Buried them in Afghani soil, nothing can grow in concrete.
Not paid to be bleeding hearts; Fucking Africa for blood diamonds!
"Most terribly sorry old chap for the mess; a slight massacre!"
'Suicide, balance of Mind disturbed'. Who's not 'disordered'?
Thank you for the warning you've been very kind.
"better strap yourself in we're landing on the surface
of the Moon's natural, last line of defence" Is it true?
"What will happen to her?" "She might make it to a
refugee camp if she's lucky & Allah will bring her peace"
"I didn't know that they were going to be murdered!"
A history of one tribe destroying another tribe; Take it as a gift!
"I can't afford to buy a gun to shoot it out." Pay us back later!
Could have all been avoided; World corruption & suffering!
Advocates of democracy; who are these real betrayers?
Who got away with murder under a Government cover up?
Person or persons unknown, cannibals of the 21st Century!
'To die for one's Country' White washed, Supreme Sacrifices.
Do you understand yet? Absolutely, No Excuses, holy warriors!
"This could be a raid." 'Smashing and Grabbing' from another.
Been here before; Under Lock Down. Absolute Devastation....
Dying for the Universe

<u>Salvador Allende - New Statue in Santiago. January 1st 2001</u>
January 29th 2001, General. Pinochet's arrest ordered, let's see!
Helicopter dumping bodies in the ocean; she was Incorrect Politically.
Where else can their Torturers retire in such dignity? Try Miami!
Need to heal our Collective Memory; Chilling Karmic generations.
Army supports today, Institution of Dictatorship, not Extraditions!
Spotlighted his fascistonista global sympathizers paying for his 5*
defence, legal posturing, Government speeches and rich lobbying.
Politicians telling the Court, 'let him go free; in our National Interest!'
The Law's an ass, he's now Incapable of standing trial, unstable, illness.
Making fantastic acts of having Alzheimer's is their defence strategy.
His shame, why? For **'Crimes Against Humanity'** - 'The Telephone!'
An Agreement of Immunity against all International Justice; it's a joke!
Dina's still in Power, now head of Police Intelligence; ghostly Chilly!
People denouncing their Amnesty, calling it the 'Kitchen' for Torture!
'Salle de Tortura'… Metal beds, Loud music to cover the screaming!
Proof of exhumed bodies: forensics' authority has no teeth for justice.
Military gave themselves Amnesty while wiring up her Vagina. WTF!!
Discovered mass graves 'the Caravan of death' with many small children.
Indicting the 'Senator for Life', he can't escape by blaming subordinates!
Tortured at the Air Force base, the infamous 'Villa Grimaldi'.
"I was someone Tortured every day and night for 3 months",
blood stuck to her body. Is this Insanity? "Forced to watch
the slow death of a young boy beaten to death with chains.
I am the only Survivor!"
'The Grill' the hangings, the drugs, 'the dry submarine'
Torturers practised Karate on his spine, cut his penis!
Psychological deepest scars. Inhuman, yet Britain Failed
to Lift the immunity! He left a long trail of blood & Agony!
Evidencia, "Companeros' screams of pain, hardest to heal.
I knew they'd torture her; unimaginable things" for a soul.
Waiting for the shocks and the beatings ~ "We'll be back!"
So much suffering, she can still be happy; feeling her spirit!
Her children will be proud because their mother is alive ~

Free Cage Browns * (eggs)
'We wouldn't do it if it wasn't bulletproof!'
Another 'mistake'; "if you break it you bought it!"
Super Psychedelic times for a Mind off the Machine.
"We have developed technology enabling Controls"
Cutting Edge – Protocols, Particle beaming.
"Whatever you do don't look at the Sun!"
*

Suicidal Fish
'Asleep walking through life' or Awake while dreaming!
Wired differently in your brain, psychomotor epilepsy.
It was an 'Accident' no such thing as 'Zero Tolerance'
Heisenberg's Principle 'Can't be 100% sure of anything'
Transported Mentally ~ changes in Self*Awareness Space.
Normal functioning, complex behaviours, automatisms, A I!
Organic brain syndrome what is the Chemical Catalyst?
Footprints in Time Waves
*

Hoping for a speed-dating Geisha from Eurasia
Pimpness the male sponsor, keeping them in line
like sleepy Caterpillars, hooking up the hookers.
'Cut to the Quick' "You make me fuckin' sick dear!"
Trippy dimensions, 'Girls with Kickstands Welcome'
Get rid of those parameters; Politics bad everywhere.
Joy passing the debacle, a body buzzing like a drill!
Uncontrollably ~ Krishna laughing
*

Petrol of Burning Bush
War not good; met her at an Islamic Rock concert
Only White boys at the Terminal on Gravity Street.
"Why apologise for the sunset, it just flows
We all owe death a Life" said Mr Rushdie.
Just one more day, accepting you will expire…
Came out and said exactly what he was thinking

*In the Garden of Eden with * a Throbbing Pineal Gland*
Caste a Cosmically ingrained hierarchy. 'Sometimes
the more intelligent You are the less you understand'
"I'll take Shakti anytime, putting it there right next to God"
"Life is Love, Love is Life" *~ Collective Consciousness.*
"You deserve to be happy and I hate goodbyes"
Let images stream at their own pace, white rabbit ~
"the Mind is harder to train than a Monkey"
"A FORM of Power that you think you don't already have!
Ain't it Amazing what Money won't buy?" A poet once sang ~
You only get a Hajji cap first time circumambulating the Kaaba.
Dreams of an overflowing vulva whirling beneath a Sufi dress.
Shiva's home, Sunrise on Ma Ganga ~ 'Om'
Free flowing streams of sub consciousness
"blood never lies"
*

Dreaming into the Present
To keep on being creative follow your passion ~ finally!
Instead of having a golden chain around your neck
of course & effect ~ the Process of living on Earth.
No one here; only an ego there if you manifest one.
Arising, remaining, passing away, growing breathing
Atomic energy with a Mind that shines out to the stars
No one there, never was never will be, Identity of illusion.
*Beginningless, beingness, multi*streams of consciousness.*
"life is a deep sleep of which love is the dream"
*

Blacking out
'Un trou de memoire'
"break up in time or die in time ~
You have to let go; that's ok darling"
Side show freak; You'd definitely go down with your ship.
Deep in the Heart
In Heaven looking down over Venus

They're Mad for It!
"I believe in All of it so None of it"
Live Art to sense ~ not just hanging on a gallery's walls.
Himalayan Radiance diffusing from Amethyst, crystal balls.
Immense transcendence high above the passes of the Hindu Kush.
As always we know nothing ~ new under this galaxy's Sun.
Coordinating collections of a mass full of diatribe ~

*

"You embraced lunatics didn't you?"
A rare creative illusion of luminosity,
no one to be fearful, selfish, ignorant,
be detached, liberated, enlightened ~ Reality.
Living in or out of a Self ~ delusional Mind-mental Shell.
That was one hell of an Amazing trip those people made.
Darling My Mind keeps getting in the way of My Heart ~
She went home and had a Ketamine Party alone. No Thanks!
Attached to the Giant of a manifested Hip Hop, Cocaine Ego.
"True freedom the most Precious Commodity on Earth"
Fertilising the Brahma Vihara

*

You sacked a thousand ships across the Milky Way.
Myths and Secrets of my Holographic Mind
Got him on a tight rope; he never came back, let's go ~
You came to me from off the walls of a Khajuraho temple
Obviously "Telling it like it is" ~ "I don't remember a thing.
Surreal glands of Russian Love travelling to bright India.
Continuum of Infinite instants, dancing through the veils
into the light beyond the horizon ~ edges off the Cortex.
Plane Rush, I'm on Right Side. 'Keep on the sunny side'
Just what she wanted; "You can make me do anything."
"Without a memory everything is new" ~ Refreshing it,
falling through the cracks, 'La Vie en Rose' and Now ~
Entanglement ~ You at the other side of the Universe.
"Deep down Inside of me I believe You Love me"

Sitting in Shiva Space

Synchronicity of a blackout ~ I was on another Planet.
I'm gonna make a phone call, get my Hookah out.
Everything, Caste's a shadow.. in the light!
Patterns inside Mother Nature ~
Patterns in the children's singing
Pattern's in your young wife's clinging
His key is a classical ADHD. opening

*

Patterns in the summer wheat fields
Patterns in the ever changing sky
Patterns in the flowing coral reefs
Patterns in Spring's blue bell dell ~
Patterns in the giant Sequoia's bark
Patterns in the stream of consciousness
Patterns of the 'me oh my!'
Patterns from my Mum and Dad & society.
Be happy, compassionate, Inspired not sad.
Realisation that I had rejected that given Program
without knowing and its consequences on my life!
Fluttering Yoni wings, twinkling, swirling, thrusting.
A great release of emotional sorrow, tears in her eyes.
Returning to my stream, threw away the shell daggers.

*

Spiral Spinal * Tapping Brain Chatter

Colour coded warnings, it was an honest mistake.
History of Acts; that flash, unadorned foresight…
'Killing because we have weapons, having weapons
because we Kill'; God shooting Vishnu ~ perpetual Love.
A Magic spell from a Magic Cunt! Spreading Star dust ~
Any Apostles 'Using a White Jesus to enslave People?'
"Dropping all your Animist beliefs from 1000's of years,
taking on the God of Your Conqueror." Freaks me out!
Sleep or dream, both the Tao ~ eternally in the here now

<u>Sparkling Speed</u>
* The Jaguar has emerald eyes *
the mermaid has Aqua-Marine eyes
the Eagle has jade eyes ~
until the Salmon never came back from Fukushima.
Newton's ~ 'Third Law of Motion' states for every
action there's an equal and opposite reaction'
Where have I heard that before?
'Stop And Search' 'Stop And Question'
'The Pass Laws', People will feel Criminalised.
Putting Words into My mouth, for which I can be Prosecuted!
Global Positioning * 7 Satellites pin-pointing where you are,
where you can shop & where You can stop & be poisoned!
Immediately, who is it 'Manufacturing Public Consent'?
'Quantum theory shows short time particles of matter
go off into different dimensions and then return'
None of it seems real in any way then you go up through
the curtain. Flying today creating more toxic emissions!
"Pick a job you love and you never work a day in your life"
Didn't get hooked, my mind's getting round it just observing.
Try Freeing your Mind. "Shut the Mind stuff up, turn it off!"
Completely Ireal but not struggling to maintain awareness ~
"Any disorders you'd like to tell us about before we begin?"
Any wonder I need these pills Doctor? UK. is Full of Paranoia!
'Echelon, Infragard, Experien'. Designing Mental environments
Law/Weapons/Words of Mass Deception/Distraction/Dirty sex
T/error\Y/our Mind\VRage in a Cage/White ain't dark Shi'ite!
A Vicious Prison cell for Your Mind
A Racist Black hole for Your Heart ~
A Solitary Dungeon for Your Intelligence
Torture chambers for your Feelings if you thought you had any!
Knowing the difference between Materialism & Infinite Spiritualism.
Knowing the difference between Computer Programs & good grass.
Operating your Mind and Awareness beyond ~ it all

"To thine own self be True" * 'Personality' of Butterfly Effects
Liberated Enlightenment ~ Transcending Your Mind-set Concept.
Sitting on a subterranean Magma bubbling up, we don't realise how
Everyone is being affected by these mental, emotional 'disorders'
Neural landscapes, Nature, all live conditioned, adapted or not to it!
All these Separated Realities darling, appearing at your front door!
It's just low levels of Dopamine in your ADHD new GM. potatoes.
Cherie after all these Years! Was it just Adrenaline frequency ~
in your Vichyssoise, releasing Fight or Flight behaviour of Fear?
Your Mania was it too much butter on the sliced white bread &
Hyperactivity the day your mother walked out the door forever
without even a goodbye! Separation Anxiety ~ dropped on you!
Instead of Jameson's let's have some Magnesium, Zinc drink
with dinner! Couldn't tolerate the loss of a secure spatial seat
in front of her favourite program on a TV. box of Opiated soap.
Anxiety Attacks something to do with his Mum's dad blowing up
at Ypres in the service of his King & Country & DNA! Lost Granny
to Agoraphobia one afternoon somewhere off the M6, Junction 9!
All the Influences, characteristics of being 'different' * same, same.
Behaviours, which affect ALL of us! (See table on pages 52 & 53)
'Egosystonic' ~ in harmony with/to the needs of the Ego
Consistent with one's Ideal (Self ~Image).
'Egodystonic' ~ dreams, impulses, compulsions, desires
in conflict, dissonant with needs/goals of the Ego.
There go I but for the Grace of God and good past karmas of empathy ~
How can anyone Judge, condemn, separate you, your Iconic influences?
Your Parents, teachers, your 1st & 2nd wives, Social Services, work rules!
Was it the stranger who said 'Hallo', your shamanic, psychedelic friend,
your best lover, a Buddhist meditation Guru? Needs some Realisation ~
that we're all effecting, living amongst, sharing Unknown, Un/Conscious
neural/behavioural patterns. Look at the list; Don't we all share some of it?
And if you don't realise it then relax with your friend who has Narcissism.
Not to make any excuses but no more Sub-Zero Tolerance ~ It is as it is.

We are a part of the whole influencing us, depending on it.
And everyone is depressed with 24/7 News, laws & Taxes.
Why wouldn't you develop all sorts of 'disorders', who makes
decisions, orders controlling your Life, from birth to the grave?
We have to give ourselves the Space by Aware Acceptance ~
not rejection of this 'sad' reality by seeing that these conditions
that are in all our deep sub-conscious DNA. can be harmonised ~
Allowed, putting them into the human*natural perspective, they're
*only attachments to this mind-body Form. **We Liberate** our selves*
letting it go realising, knowing we have essence which is Cosmic.
Allowance ~ that is who we truly are together, the rest are just
indeterminable patterns, algorithms, radiant magnetic Sun rays.
We are Fine Tuning ~ this endless list by not attaching, bonding
ourselves to this 'movie' but listening to Krishna's divine flute ~
Making some connection, society values our unconsciousness by
not seeing our true essence, their behaviour is blind cause & effect.
Karmic seeds * reacting to the Ignorance of underlying conditioning.
*Effects of a System giving us our sense of Self*Selfishness or **Spirit?***
Living in Island gated communities doesn't help the Paranoia brother,
have to transcend and open up knowing it's all delusions of y/our mind!
Custodial Warranty... Virtually 'Locked In.. Ego what is your own Image?
Dealing with your stuttering, passive aggression, ADHD & other people's
***Expectations**! Divorce didn't help her anorexia; the biased courts took my*
daughter away based on a story of lies from one I loved, who betrayed me!
Silent, sitting in a cell, post traumatic stress disorder inside a Golden Pagoda.

*

Chemical Sheep of Reading Gaol
Enlarge Your Spirit Grow ~ Your Spirit not on a tread mill mate.
Off-duty do it yourself before the Storm troopers get to your door.
Divorced they found a body of Self-deconstruction. Pics. off DNA.
sequences, strings and hypnotised, sociopathic destruction profile.
Every Guru helping you knows it (limited body*Mind disorders).
You are eternal ~ everyone you meet is inside you Sat Guru.
Sensational feelings * Lotuses unfolding inside your heart

Undercurrent of Life Stream

'In Buddhist psychology the process of the changing mind is manifested in two levels or streams. The sub-conscious stream **'Bhavanga Citta'** and the conscious stream **'Vithi citta'**. Each one merges into the other. The sub-conscious stream is a hidden repository of all the impressions and memories of thoughts that pass through the conscious mind; All experiences and tendencies are stored up there, but they exert an influence over the conscious mind without it being aware of the source of this influence. These two streams of mind being conditioned by each other. The state of the active conscious mind and awareness is generally present during the day when one is awake. It is conscious of all impacts and impressions continually received from outside, through the five senses or of sensations received from within by way of ideas or thoughts or recollections of former thoughts. When this conscious stream which is constantly receiving sensations from within or without subsides into inactivity, as for instance during sleep, the other stream, the sub-conscious (Bhavanga Citta) manifests, flowing like an undisturbed stream so long as the conscious stream does not arise to disturb it through the sense channels. When awake every time an arisen thought of the conscious mind subsides and before the next thought can arise within that infinite-simally minute fraction of time, the sub-conscious stream intervenes. Then when the next thought of the conscious mind level arises the sub-conscious stream subsides into inactivity. Since innumerable thoughts arise and fall one after another during the day so then are there innumerable momentary interruptions to the flow of the sub-conscious stream during the day. The sub-conscious is referred to as a state of subliminal activity, viz. an activity that takes place below the threshold of the conscious mind, an activity of which therefore there is no awareness on the conscious mind.

The conscious stream holds only one thought or idea at a time
whereas the sub-conscious stream holds all the impressions of all the
thoughts ideas and experiences that enter and leave the conscious mind.
This sub-conscious life stream allows us to have a memory,
conditioning our thinking and action.
The Bhavanga is the 'bhava' (existence) & 'anga' (factor)
'Bhavanga Citta' is the indispensable factor or basis of existence.
The factor of life by means of which the flow of existence or being is
maintained without a break, the continuing basis or undercurrent
of life, the stream of existence keeping life going. This stream
of being is an indispensable condition of individual life.
It is comparable to the current of a river when it flows
calmly on, unhindered by any obstacle, and when that
current is opposed by any thought from the world within or
perturbed by tributary streams of the senses from the world
without then thoughts in the conscious mind stream arise.
There is a juxtaposition of momentary states of consciousness
subliminal and supra-subliminal throughout a lifetime'.

*

From 'Rebirth Explained'
by V. Gunaratna.
Buddhist Publication Society, Kandy, Sri Lanka. 1980
This essential conscious ~ sub-conscious life stream is felt
as a flow of sensations on the body/mind; an equanimous
awareness of this ever changing flow of energy, sensations.
'Sampaggana Satimo' is 'Vipassana Insight Meditation'
(as taught by S N Goenkaji, www.dhamma.org)
Used in practice to make us realise our true Inner, omniscient, Cosmic being.
(putting 'y/our disorders' into an 'undefined', beyond Mind, Spiritual context).
See, Buddhist Publishing Society, 'The Four Sublime States'
Nyanaponika Maha Thera

A*: Acquired Epileptiform Aphasia, Acute Disseminated Encephalomyelitis, Adrenoleukodystrophy, Agenesis of the corpus callosum, Agnosia, Aicardi syndrome, Alexander disease, Alpers' disease, Alternating hemiplegia, Alzheimer's disease, Amyotrophic lateral sclerosis (see Motor Neurone Disease), Anencephaly, Angelman syndrome, Angiomatosis, Anoxia, Aphasia, Apraxia, Arachnoid cysts, Arachnoiditis, Arnold-Chiari malformation, Arteriovenous malformation Asperger's syndrome, Ataxia Telangiectasia, Attention Deficit Hyperactivity Disorder, Autism, Auditory processing disorder, Autonomic Dysfunction.*

B: *Back Pain, Batten disease Behcet's disease, Bell's palsy, Benign Essential Blepharospasm, Benign Focal Amyotrophy, Benign intracranial hypertension Bilateral frontoparietal polymicrogyria, Binswanger's disease, Blepharospasm, Bloch-Sulzberger syndrome, Brachial plexus injury Brain abscess, Brain damage, Brain injury, Brain tumor, Spinal tumor, Brown-Sequard syndrome.*

C: *Canavan disease, Carpal tunnel syndrome(CTS), Causalgia Central pain syndrome, Central pontine myelinolysis, Centronuclear myopathy, Cephalic disorder, Cerebral aneurysm, Cerebral arteriosclerosis, Cerebral atrophy, Cerebral gigantism, Cerebral palsy, Charcot-Marie-Tooth disease, Chiari malformation, Chorea, Chronic inflammatory demyelinating polyneuropathy (CIDP), Chronic pain, Chronic regional pain syndrome, Coffin Lowry syndrome, Coma, includes Persistent Vegetative State, Congenital facial diplegia, Corticobasal degeneration, Cranial arteritis, Craniosynostosis, Creutzfeldt-Jakob disease, Cumulative trauma disorders, Cushing's syndrome, Cytomegalic inclusion body disease (CIBD), Cytomegalovirus Infection.* ***D:*** *Dandy-Walker syndrome, Dawson disease, De Morsier's syndrome, Dejerine-Klumpke palsy, Dejerine-Sottas diseaseDementia, Dermatomyositis, Developmental Dyspraxia, Diabetic neuropathy, Diffuse sclerosis, Dysautonomia, Dyscalculia, Dysgraphia, Dyslexia, Dystonia*

E: *Early infantile epileptic encephalopathy ~ The 'identification' of 'disorders' that puts you in a talking box, a captive of your Mind.*

*Empty sella syndrome, Encephalitis, Encephalocele,
Encephalotrigeminal angiomatosis, Encopresis, Epilepsy,
Erb's palsy Essential tremor, Erythromelalgia, **F:** Fabry's disease,
Fahr's syndrome, Fainting, Familial spastic paralysis, Febrile seizures,
Fisher syndrome, Friedreich's ataxia **G:** Gaucher's disease,
Gerstmann's syndrome, Giant cell arteritis, Giant cell inclusion
disease, Globoid cell, Leuko- dystrophy, Gray matter heterotopia,
Guillain-Barré syndrome **H:** HTLV-1 associated myelopathy,
Hallervorden - Spatz disease, Head injury, Headache, Hemifacial
Spasm, Hereditary Spastic Paraplegia, Heredopathia atactica
polyneuritiformis, Herpes zoster oticus, Herpes zoster, Hirayama
syndrome, Hypoxia, Holoprosencephaly, Huntington's disease,
Hydranencephaly, Hydrocephalus, Hypercortisolism
I: Immune-Mediated encephalomyelitis, Inclusion body myositis,
Incontinentia pigmenti, Infantile phytanic acid storage disease,
Infantile Refsum disease, Infantile spasms, Inflammatory myopathy,
Intracranial cyst, Intracranial hypertension **J:** Joubert syndrome.
K: Kearns-Sayre syndrome, Kennedy disease, Kinsbourne syndrome,
Klippel Feil syndrome, Krabbe disease, Kugelberg-Welander disease,
Kuru **L:** Lafora disease, Lambert -Eaton myasthenic syndrome, Landau
- Kleffner syndrome, Lateral medullary (Wallenberg) syndrome,
Learning disabilities, Leigh's disease, Lennox-Gastaut syndrome,
Lesch-Nyhan syndrome, Leukodystrophy, Lewy body dementia
Lissencephaly Locked-In syndrome, Lou Gehrig's disease (Motor
Neurone Disease), Lumbar disc disease, Lyme disease - Neurological
Sequelae **M:** Machado-Joseph disease, (Spinocerebellar ataxia type 3)
Macrencephaly, Megalencephaly Melkersson-Rosenthal syndrome,
Menieres disease, Meningitis, Menkes disease Metachromatic
leukodystroph, Microcephaly, Migraine Miller Fisher syndrome, Mini-
Strokes, Mitochondrial Myopathies, Mobius syndrome, Monomelic
amyotrophy, Motor Neurone Disease, Motor skills disorder, Moyamoya
disease, Muco-polysaccharidoses, Multi-Infarct Dementia, Multifocal
motor neuropathy, Multiple sclerosis, Multiple system atrophy
Your vibration in the higher spiritual realm beyond a body of disorders.*

<u>How to come to me</u>
All the Material world, the good & bad from the Cosmic.
The Transcendental Pleasures, sowing a natural seed
in the deepest heart of the living entity.
"One travels throughout the Universe before he is fortunate
enough to meet an intelligence who transmits
Transcendental seeds of devotion which fructifies when it pierces
the Material Universe into the effulgence of light ** Spiritual sky **

*

<u>In the heart of every atom</u>
Beyond Man's reasoning powers, understanding ~
Absolute Truth; Teaching the philosophy of devotion.
Plants growing flowers under the Lotus feet of Krishna
fully absorbed ~ as a fish lives in water.
Engaged in Transcendental loving even poorest of poor
Offering their genuine love ~ simplicity,
the leaf of a flower

*

<u>Heron Spirit ~ Not for a Program</u>
"Colours for measuring Space"
Atmospheric Painting
'Olive & Mustard'
'Yellow & Rose'
'Orange, lemon & Violet'
'Reds with Green Emerald discs, in a synchronised field'
with Imaginary, Incandescent Skies & Vertical light.
Stripes and bands of Visual language * Unique Images
Sensations for your Sensuous Awareness to make 'Real'
'Tradition, patterns, textures, colour, size, tone, line.
Created Cubist grammar, Illusions of perspective ~
Bending planes of colour, rendering Forms in deep space.
How not to lose the abstractness of an Image.'
Simply dreams floating out of an open window ~
Liberation of sub-conscious rainbow frequencies

Look at the Stars our Reality is Enormous
It is Mind creating everything in the Material World
Fine Tuning the Universal energy existing in you ~
Consciousness of your body is through the senses
Transcending them, be liberated from all Conditioning..
'The disorders', habits, identifications and their Effects.
Your Mind has given too much power to the syndromes'
frequencies you have, don't have, might have, the same
same with people around you and even far off strangers!
Have tolerance & empathy, much is unknown (90%) in Us!
What is effecting our primeval original sub-consciousness?
This ever changing energy you can't control its destiny ~
So much we can never know about our Universe, using
10% of the brain and how is that vital organ responding
to Visible & Invisible shock waves pervading the Tao ~
Being in the here & now, Gautama took a rest and bow
from torturing himself to find an answer to this enigma.
This sub-conscious reaction (see pp. 50-51) bubbling up
with the next 'disorder' to influence the attention of y/our
ever changing Mind & body outside our 'defined' states.
Move on ~ transmute, put it into perspective, be free ~
I'm allowing myself to live, drop into the next dimension.
The boundlessness of the whole experience shines a light
giving us our 'Sense of Reality' and who each of us is ~
You stuck to it, suffered it to an unbearable end, Ego/Mind
wasn't helping, just repeating the patterns, never lets it go!
You gave it its chance but same old obsession getting worse.
Time's moving on ~ park the Mind's dictates and let it flow.
Now say enough, no separateness to all inclusive beingness
Not Brain Dead; living in a Digital Democratic Cage; engage!
The body is your Temple of Sense Consciousness to realize.
You are your Spaceship beaming to your Self ~ Inner Sat Guru.
Omnipotent, Omnificent, Omnipresent, Omniscience, Omkar

Why not find your 'Inner Guru' and Tune in first?
Strong grip ~ being happy but with no attachment soul mate.
Natural harmony is detached, equilibrium in your cerebellum,
bursting! Capitalism conditions people to crave not rave,
fulfilling their Addictions, deep roots to all the bondages ~
So you have to spend more to feed unsatisfied desires,
it's how the Economy works stupid! We sold those Weapons,
WMD of Mass Destruction! The biggest suppliers to the World!
Every consumer needs a dealer, needs a supplier NWO. gringo.
How do you afford to feed your wife, your BMW & pay high taxes?
Educated in greed, desire, jealousy, envy, dissatisfaction & more...
Who's keeping score on your debts watching you?
Britain's debt is more than their GNP. (Independent 27/08/2007).
We needed to 'Make' an Empire of Power to Feed our God King.
Learning how to Manipulate the Mind's innate expectation.
You taught me selfishness, rejection, denial, disdain, haughtiness,
if you didn't get what you wanted. (US & UK have the most divorces
in the world plus the biggest private prison populations of the west).
Over capacities
*

Seeing Beyond Your Own Limited Mind for what it is ~ 'I Am'*'It Is'
'Mrs Bhutto, who left in 1999 to avoid arrest; wants to return to be
Prime Minister of Pakistan and said that outstanding charges of
corruption were "No longer a stumbling block." Why, who said that?
Now unfortunately she's been assassinated by another bunch of nutters!
Life's Celebration not compulsive Obsession, power of crude Addiction!
Its **Ego free**, immune, in fine tune, free of hate, greed, repression,
no autocratic political correctness; free spirits float in entanglement.
Liberation from your Manias, recognising the Maniacs around you;
Aware, Realising, surrendering, witness, sorry too late ~ Inshallah.
Jumping off the plank, let the fears go into clear Crystal waters.
'Whatever s/he wants to be,' added to your short term memory.
Not interested in any responsibility for your high maintenance
being, caught in so many machinations of Ignorant Corruption

TAO
Your Kisses broke me
Free

It's not philosophy it's common sense ~
"You're Innocent, we're children, free spirits"
Some people need to possess and manipulate!

*

In the Dock

Defendant what's your name? Some people call me, Walking On Sunshine ~
I'm a Natural Living Man not a dead person or a Government Collateralised slave.
Therefore I want my Rights so help me God, your Authority has no jurisdiction.
Famous for all the wrong reasons, getting interest paid from my birth, a fraud!
They're all lying bastards, the whole game is a massive deceit and
he's been groomed, a stooge, getting the blame for starting WW111
"What you don't Know can't hurt you", who said that?
"If you've got nothing to hide you got nothing to fear"
Krishna's dancing on the heads of clever illusions

*

Causeless Mercy Never a Victim.

Hanuman, "Which direction on the battlefield?"
Already dead but will always exist in time & space.
Sounded their transcendental conch shells of Victory
Riding on Agni's Surreal blazing*Chariot of a fire God.
'Controlling' all the transcendental senses ~
Taking shelter in the 'Supreme' with nothing, no fears…
Cosmic Alchemy ~ Up & down, juggler of golden spheres.
Weakness of his Mind, a slave to excessive Attachments ~
The loss of Mental Equilibrium ~ of any Conditioned Soul.
My lover's on this Material Plane, we give each other
Pleasure. Insane out of our realities, rules of lustful,
fecund activities, attracting elemental energies…
of our passionate bodies in devotional life ~
Our hearts entered into the Sun's orbit

Vishnu's Non Self-Interest
Unarmed & unresisting allowed to go free ~
Cast aside your bow & arrows darling
Your soft heart of devotions receives Self*Knowledge
"Don't ask what Mother Earth can Do for You
but What You can do for Mother Earth."
Natural balance ~ the Pendulum stopped!
Sounds better than blasting Blue Whales into a billion bits.
Incoming ~ Cosmic psychic channels bypassing Taiji Bay!
*
Dropped on my head a different logic
Torture is now called 'Stress Techniques' 'Harsh Interrogation'
For Sanitized Minds in USA; How many hits for killing Insects?
Definition, 'Police State', 'Zero Tolerance'; not allowing us to grow!
And a quick bullet to the head is called 'friendly fire'. "Sorry mate"
Impacts on our children, our seeds, on our nerve cells, the future!
Head of the Inquisition looking at your social media, hard drives!
Free of Virtual imprisonment, 'thoughts' in Your Mind ~
'The world's most dangerous animal, Anopheles mosquito'
'Professor Zwiebel's research provides a biologic context and
then strips it down to a few molecular targets that we are using
to develop chemical modifiers that should have direct impacts on
mosquito's behaviour". To Obey or Not to Obey? Witnessing it all.
We shouldn't have come out the trees; nature of Mind, No Mind stuff!
*
Sold a pup & a pig in the poke
The long embrace, "I'm trying to ~ "
"Putting it out of your mind and heart!"
'To believe or not to believe' 'To Obey or Not to Pay'
Knowing the Materialistic & Spiritual Realties authenticity ~
Subtle, not subtle ~ in multi * dimensional transcendence
What, It is what it is ~ It is what it isn't is..
'Sharing Love is all we need'

Waiting to Die, Why?
"What's the sound of a feeling?"
What's the deep colour of a feeling
what's the taste of a feeling
what's the smell of a feeling
what's the touch of a feeling
what's the thought of a feeling
"knowledge is Pain" ~ lucidity!
"Don't you know the Rules anymore?"
"You can't force a woman against her will"
She saved him from his own Self destruction.
Infinite Space is a long time ~ Away from You.
"Is this not the time for Love?" Carefree winds ~
Translating the upheaval into a painting, of the revolution.
Free spirit, "In command of the conventions" ~ releasing them.
"His Landscapes are Mindscapes" His crazy hallucinations on fire.
Swaying wheat fields filled with mood swings of squawking crows!
Welcome to the lemon fluorescence of an Arlesian Night Café.
Living with the inevitability of another unprovoked 'disorder'!
Through chemical imbalance, held onto some Inspired Revelation.
Deeply wild, cherished beauty gone forever and ever in a fever ~
Infinity is a vast Ocean for a 'diagnosed' epileptic to transcend but..
"I knew you would" ~ Unbearable pain losing your Sunflowers.
"You're destroying the thing you Love"
It's all Your fault, You must die; reaction to fear!
You're going to leave with him; a dagger in his heart…
"You forced me to kill you!" "I didn't know what else to do!"
Autumn leaves, degeneration into golden sunsets, nature's originality
moment to moment ~ inspiration of a vortex spinning in your mind.
Transcending 'disability' ~ Vincent lives within his neural paintings.
I can see the music, taste your touch, smell the wind, hear your
emotions, feeling your dreams. In tune with genuine pigments,
Indian Yellow was created from the urine of cows fed mango leaves.

It Dies * Transmuting

Turn that energy in the right direction ~
by getting detached from the wrong direction, thing.
Love is only for the Divine being forever ~ changing.
Nobody's desires are fulfilled so you want a rebirth.
Trapped by your own free-will, it's called MAYA.
She is the Goddess' energy of all your Illusions ~
and desires, impossible to resist her in your mind.
Maya doesn't disturb the meditation of Shiva ~
Although she's always trying to get his attention.

*

Ramana Maharshi

"You are the unmoving one. Problems will be endless
so long as one is not aware of it. If you Identify yourself
with the body you are bound to dualities.
The Mind keeps wandering as in dreams"

*

No Class A's

So high on life! You're dosing down your life ~
Ambition: 'To make Myself Happy in Life' (for the best of all).
We're starving, what can you do? Nobody gives a shit about you!
Kids hunting with Black Kites living off the Kolkata scrap heaps.
"Just lookin' for a bit of membrane" what happened to eternal life?
"There go I but for the Grace of God." Do you know what I mean?

*

Pandit Bandit

"He can't judge anyone else ~ Mr. Celebrity, virtual Pundit.
He should be detached from all of this if he really knows!"
Mind controlling mind, what we're all told to believe...
"Guru, why should I want to read anyone else's mind?
Maybe he's going into more Maya, why be led there?
Why follow anyone, follow your own instincts ~
There can be guides but You have to do it!"
Wisdom of the Heart

Space Beyond the Neocortex

We've all got something of everything, no guilt, blame or shame.
Got the Sun in my eyes, being Real as a life consciousness.
Doctrine (BG ch 18.59): 'to have to go and fight for God'.
He washed the fear out of him and showed him again…
Never expected to hear any of this in the Celestial Song.
How to improve your 'Detention Techniques' of Torture.
Don't be carried away by the false Ego of the body-mind.
His Natural duty, to fight for justice ~ Krishna's ascendency.
God's instruction not Arjuna's bad Karma; be another Osama?
Finding the true motivation; forgetfulness of a conditioned soul.
(BG ch.18.61) Supreme Lord in every heart is directed by him.
Transcendental by surrendering your 'disabled' Mind-set Form.
Haven't been able to accept this doctrine yet; still being human
and compassionate, able to reject war! I can Celebrate my life!
I can look myself in the mirror and be happy with who I am.
I never reached this level of philosophy of being ~ detached.
Truly accepting what you can, living with who you are openly.
Being a discoverer or falling under false illusions. 'I know ~
'I' can transcend this material reality through 'Vipassana'
Without giving enemies lethal injections, although I might!
Live a naturally balanced life not as a compulsive obsessive

*

Spirituality
Materially free ~
of Time * Space
Transcendentally

*

'Dreams Are Good
their Reality Is even better.'
Passively ~ sitting by a river
Challenging my Mind to witness.
Creating Inspirational insight

La Concha

That unique sperm ~ right time * right place…
Expectation ~ setting Your*self up, for a fall, caught in time!
So many options with manipulations. "Get A Grip" be Aware ~
Understanding Celestial songs, swimming within orbital red dwarfs,
tempted two Tuscany sisters at a black moon party, Koh Pha Ngan.
Getting the indications, feelings, vibrations, smiles, sweet smell,
spirals from the divine proportions of her smooth, rosy, shell
*

Fell into her 12 strand DNA; jetting over Venus Bay.
Body cells giving off her codes, helixes & formulae ~
Consciousness serenading me, freedom in a frequency
falling deep inside earthly magnetic vortices, beautiful sex.
Not attracting negative energies, becoming evolutionaries
*

Her Cosmic light spreading photons, my encoded rays.
Infusion of shining, spiralling, generating spatial DNA *
Potential of Sirius & Venus' * sacred Tantric conjunctions.
Electro-magnetic energies, bright reflecting burning filaments.
Updating nervous systems of creation ~ refiguring Functions.
Awakening dormant brain cells into multi-dimensionality ~
Chakras enlightening your memory bank ~ remembering
Who You Are
*

Releasing genetic, Ignorant dramas into Universal seasons.
Attraction, hooked together in Our Love * Astral destinies.
Triggering changes of thought ~ vibrations for the Planet
Extending imaginary boundaries ~ into infinite Galaxies.
Seeding your Cosmic womb with Psychic sperm intuitions.
Imprints coming * from Star systems,
through cellular kisses
All pulsating throbbing

Conqueror's Freedom
'You're Free not to have your house, wife and children again!
Our gift to you for free from a democracy gone fully insane.'
'He was proud in that he disdained those who loved him!'
Plantain grows in pure gravel, an amazing little plant
Pulls the nutrients out of the rock, pulls the toxins out of you.
"Some call it a weed"

*

Transmitting the Thoughts
You have to let go as that person....
Otherwise you're UNFORMLESS in a prison!
C O N S C I O U S N E S S
But your Mind makes you believe a lot of things.
Trained to believe the Mind is Inside You ~
You are Inside the Big phantom Mind!
'Thoughts' are coming in Cosmically.
Learn to transcend the Big Mind ~
Shiva's Space beyond Time Itself

*

Bring it on * Full Astral * Projection
I'm on the corner of 2 days, felt like turning the page.
I could see the music foster a sense of marvel in you
Regeneration & Disentanglement, no more hyperlinks.
"An eye for eye * makes the whole World blind." Gandhi.
Golden Eagles transcending gravity, high in the sky with
soaring Albatrosses and falcons with the eyes of Horus.
"All great changes are based on pain and destruction?"

*

Wrapped in a Protective Straight Jacket
"Man Up" they're Watching out for you!
Watching over you >Watching You >for Your Own Protection
<YOU > Why don't you Protect that fragile Burmese democracy?
Not Allowing the Nobel Peace laureate to be kept inside a prisoner.
'Insein Jail' > Not Killing the light * even for a moment ~

"Tomorrow Never Comes" (for Nano Sea Cucumbers)
"Hate fuels Resistance", Dr. Leary, #1 most wanted by the FBI;
CIA & a Democracy and culture of Insanity. Dysfunctionality!
'50,000 Iraqi people fleeing their country each month'
"They want to destroy any kind of personal freedom"
An order was given and they were forced to Obey.
Escaping to the frontier, holding a Kaaba souvenir in dismay.
Hiding out with smoking prophets in thorny Blackberry bushes
Bringing 'Passive Infra Red Motion Detectors' into Operation
Surveillance by the Military Industrial Complex in your local!
Didn't you read the writing on the wall? Only saw bullet holes
'At same time Memory manipulated within a cage of energy'
"Light and non light is the language of the Universe"
Found a baby in 'Packeteer' binary codes translating her Pin.
You don't know you're a Victim until Now ~ gratitude for life!
Theory of energy deflection, reflection, diffraction, refractions.
Your entire Cosmic field is present, beingness ~ not Mind stuff!
Magma bubbles bubbling in subterranean, sub-consciousness.
Are you a Meditator trying to get somewhere on a true path ~?
Dropping off an edge, falling into Space, being blissed by Grace.
Effecting your reactions, behaviour, affecting your moods and mine!
Who wouldn't be off their rocker with this shit to contend with Dr?

*

A Name for Another Very Long Trail of Tears/Fears
"If you don't have the bombs to back it up; Keep Walking"
'Dragon-Fly' camera*recorders at Anti-War protests in NY.
Can't outrun helicopters, radio or Cosmic aura retroviruses,
on the 'Reservation' or in a 'Concentrated Refugee Camp'!
"God is never more Popular than in Times of War"
Robert Ardrey, "Guns speak Louder than words" Mr. Cochise
Keep walkin' too; 'Guess we better dig a bigger hole for him!'
Understanding non Materialism inside Esoteric Architecture.
Absorbing Wonderlust & Wander*lost ~ proportional Vibrations

"Who You Calling Uncivilised?" ~ Fred C Dobbs
"We've already found Life's Real Treasure, darling"
Species Thesis, the Program for Organic Agricultural.
Swimming upstream left us a Pointer, have to be free to Love.
Your Own Truth, Making things happen
What's Real You Know?
You Are going to leave Your body ~
"In Control of Your Own Life!" On your trip.
People Are Oblivious to this Controlling System.
Jesus stood Up, broke the bonds! Believe IT Just IS
A Computer Generated Game called Brain.
Digital Life & Death ~ the New Cosmic Program...
Pin Codes 10110110' ~ Turning off the switch & signs.
Machines running down digital, energetic, telepathic lines.

*

Agent Smith We'll Pull the Plug!
Getting Faster and Faster
Focus on Shiva ~ being Shiva
A Prison of Your Mind
It can't be True - Why Not?
Making a Choice (Teddy bear pill/Red pill)
Helping to Free the Mind
'Load Us Up!'

*

*Viruses * from Heaven*
I designed the Beautiful Girl in the Crimson Dress.
'Digital Pimp' - Machines Thinking for the Humans.
Evolution of whose Future? Power Plants..
Hacking into the Mind, his Alpha patterns.
*Into the Main Frame * Into the Main Frame.*
Your 'Thinking' Program, the Most Powerful Program.
Fields of Fusion - Evade the SYSTEM, the Paranoia.
7 digit password, Sign In, Existing User, Put Username.
No Silicon tits in Atlantis

<u>Digital environment*Digital reality</u>
be ~ 'Super Rich' Materialist through digital brain Programming.
Creative Intelligence, chemicals, powers of electro-magnetism.
The bio-feedback, being the Cosmic connections.
**** We're Inside a Computer residual ****
Mental Projection, algorithms of Your Digital Self
What Is Real ~ What You Can Feel * IN SPACE
Electrical signals Interpreted by your cerebral cortex
Now neural Interactive Simulation, connecting to a Cloud.
Being Made to Live in a Dream World of Stimulation.
"Your On Line Service is Operating Normally"

*

<u>I Want the Love Program</u>
Wake the fuck Up - Regeneration on another level
Seeing, Being "A Part of Everything"
Feeling the Electro Magnetic pulse of an ant.
Can't Wait any longer….

*

Computer Generated Virtual World of Brain/Mind/Condition.
Mental-Forms living within a Body of Sense Consciousness.
Keeping Humans Under Control, Step this way, take a shower!
The Mind has trouble letting go ~ Possessed in a Slave market!
Saw Them with My own Eyes, the Planets (matrix)
Take your pick, buy a ticket, Mr. Philip K Dick.
Enter Any Program * No Key to Press Escape.
'Breaking Gravity ~ If You Can, bending the Sea.
All In the Mind, the Cosmos, the Universal, Dreams ~
The Infinite Space, arousing hot desires in your screams.
Living to Your Maximum Power * Orgasms by All Means!
Releasing these **'disorders'**~ Free Your Mind, simply be.
I can only show you the door, don't pretend to be blind.
'How to Operate in this Reality' with new 'Realisation'
Get the feeling ~ You have to let it all go by yourself.
Being your Infinite, No Limits ~ 'Om Namah Shivaya'

Be happy forever
On levels we don't understand but welcome the stars.
Manifesting a 3 D. interpretation of your own mind.
* Stones put together with Astronomical meaning *
You think about something differently … You're there.
Bathing in the flowing river of one thousand light lingams ~
The media hacking into your brain! The richest 8 people now
have as much wealth as half the Planet's population. Pardon?
You can never have too much! Recently it came down from 62
Barons; there's Gold everywhere! Do what your heart tells you.
10 million kip fine for smoking a joint!
Life is a trip hang on!
*
Myanmar Resonating in the Stupa with Camp Nama
Who's your friend in the Obsessional, Compulsive tin hat?
The monks are all gone, we don't know where they are ~
Only the Army's in the Schwedagon Temple; leader of Junta
Than Shwe is kicked out the UN; dictatorship just like in Tibet!
Corrupt, despotic, tyrannical Generals have ruined a dhamma
land rich in natural resources and the World sat back obliviously.
The Regime covers up its atrocities and good old USA threatens
unspecified sanctions on Yangon but has lost all its credibility!
Covertly, soldiers only coming at night, secret trials and tortures.
The Opposition died under interrogation; so we can't complain!
Ethics drugged, blindfolded, handcuffed in solitary Confinement
at Al Ghraib, Guantanamo Bay. Smuggled out monks' testimony
on small memory sticks & She's disappeared…
*
Sampling * Rebellion
"We have the power to resist the constant message of fear"
Using Technology to Improve Life, easy but the elite's fucked it up!
Our decisions ~ Up to us, looking Into Our Own Hearts and Minds.
Keeping Us Free, is this what's called 'Democracy' based in Love ~

<u>Visionary*No Darkness</u>
"Protecting one's Privacy - Attitude to Authority's Forces!"
1960's sign of Great Britain, looking for a 'Room To Rent'
'No Blacks, No Dogs, No Irish' ~ (No Children in the 80's!)
*1st Race Riot * Petrol Bombs in Notting Hill, London, 1958.*
Found 236 New Planets, 28th May 2007 ~ being Now
*

<u>Our Relationships, Common Sense, Choices Now</u>
War of T/error or www.planetfriendly.net, beinghuman.com?
What is Your true Nature? Ask the Black Pope if he knows!
*FREE WILL * FREE CHOICE * FREE SPIRIT* CONSCIOUSLY.*
Making a choice about what sort of World, life do you/we want.
What Leadership In the Future? FREEDOM IS FUNDAMENTAL
or the Pass Laws, being Sectioned with one signature. Whose?
Our Sense of Powerful > Powerlessness < WHY? Ask the Jesuits.
*

Our Leaders entered into the Sociopathic, 'Politics of Fear' Why?
"We are being Watched and Controlled without Our Knowledge..."
"Little broad based Objection gave up to Cynicism and distraction;
Negativities!" How do You let that affect Your Life and environment?
What are Your Influences; Picasso's inspiration for painting Guernica!
Now No Spiritual Meaning, staged Media events, everything feels False.
www.care2.com. ('Manufacturing Consent', Dr. Chomsky I presume?).*
Do you want/need more Personal Security of a Straight Jacket Reality?
Being suited up for Your Own Protection brother. WHY?
Have You lost Your Sense/Instinct/memory of Freedom?
"You don't need to watch everyone if everyone believes
they're being watched. Punishment isn't necessary but
the inevitability of punishment has to be programmed
into the brain."

We've moved onto a New Threat (Now forgotten the lies of WMD)
"Fear encourages Intolerance, Racism, Xenophobia. Fear creates
the need for a constant series of symbolic actions manufactured
by the authorities to show that; Yes they are protecting us,
from all possible dangers!"

*

'Being told what to think got us into trouble in the 1ˢᵗ place!'
Specific fears are created & sustained by the Media; Wham!
Manipulation - Constant Messaging of Impending disasters.
Hooked into Ego ~ Destruction, Violence, Crime, Falseness.
Effects of this Insecurity on our World View; diabolical, evil.
Getting your Audiences' Attention > Stand by for Station
Identification and 'A WORD FROM OUR SPONSORS'
You have been Targeted by a Cyber-Predator & Worse!

*

Immediate & Remote Corrosiveness
'Not everyone can pay for their TV. license in one go'.
Need to have some Laws (and how to enforce them?).
Tipping the Human/environ/mental/Spiritual balance to
Extremes. 'Remote Control' > Sensors for our Senses!
Fear is part of our survival instinct programmed into our
neurological system, 'the Internet is multiplying Psy-Ops
warfare's sources of Information. These threats are Real!'
Shows how many of us Live In 'This Global Culture Of Fear'
Control > Virtually taking away all Our Trust; My Good son.
In the Machine System & in $ We Trust so help me, WHY?
Where did you get your Memories & Judgments & feelings?
Values, realities, reactions from the brain of a Blade Runner!
Vipassana tells us this reaction is 'disordered' cause & effect,
which is determining our Karma in our sub-conscious Mind.
Continuing the vicious cycles; wheels of Ignorance not Bliss.
Need to become self-aware of sensations ~ of life processes.
'Nama/rupa' and **be here now** *liberated; just is, beingness ~*
Seeing this coercive programming working on my parents…

"Live simply so that others may simply live" - M. Gandhi
Met Sam Hain on the way to a Celtic New Year Party.
"Have You Lost Your Mind?" Slaves are outlawed!
The delusional World has been pulled over your eyes
'A Prison for Your Mind' Wake Up brother and sister!
Like the Gestapo goose-stepping into Byelorussia.
Going into Arrest, bit of a Very Rude Awakening!
Seeing it for your*self ~ take a trip to Wonderland.
Hometown: 'Over the Rainbow' on the blue coast

*

Bugged with a Bug

"let me give you one piece of advice" ~ 'be true'
"You know something but you can't explain it"
"If you have a touch phone; Press Star 1 now ~
"Our Informers are there to Protect Your white arse".
All this Gestapo stuff, with the help of super computers!
Who's in Charge?
Whose Mind – Program, app, cloud is being used?
Giving up your rights, already given up your DNA...
What if their information is wrong, not a true profile?
Not used for Your benefit and they want you! ~ Did you
see Mr. Menezes in Stockwell tube, never came back up!

*

Good Timing

An idiot's Policy. Protecting their own servile Careers.
'Need Privacy to Vote, to make Love, to talk to God' or
a sexy Angel or simply a person of goodness, like Diego
Rivera's flower seller of Calla lilies or Antonio the gardener.
Do I have the honesty to look them in the eyes?
Want to see the whole package, climbing up the walls in Varanasi!
Some people burn incense to TB. gods, No doubt.
Give me the injection!
Honouring or Ignoring
LOVE TO LOVE

'Life is not separate to death. It only looks that way'
~ Blackfoot Indian Proverb

*

They say when a baby's in its mother's womb it gets
her smell which it will remember for the rest of its life.
More to life than what this 10% tells us or thinks it knows.
"No one likes it, everyone puts up with it" ~ Why Professor?
Enjoying the company of Radha, representation of humanity.
Not bonded, possessive; In love with your mother's free spirit.
Transcending time ~ space, no form but you've got your body.
Enjoy your life, be happy, be balanced, be conscious, relax,
do your best, be a poet, be a father.

*

Binary/2 way switching Mind * /0/1/0/1/0/1/0' ~
+ - On Off, like dislike back forward order 'disorder'
happiness and sadness in this materialist reality of ~
passion, desire, joy, grief, life, death, processing of instants.
Knowing more of the experiences of being ~ it's learning.
Be light hearted, let go ~ swim with translucent Angel fish
You're not a vowed monk, enjoy being humanity on Earth.
'Know the difference between materialism and spiritualism'
Alive ~ feel your heart, let it smile inside & outside freely

*

Aware*ness
Keeping tabs on anyone who appears not to belong here.
Realise; being ~ Monitored without our Consent, brother.
*Schwab, **'Feel valued no matter how much you're worth'***
Ad/ "The motive was literature not tourism or to escape"
Now we're able to see our Planet Earth from a distance!

*

Angel Icon, Joannie Mitchel.
'Drop the Ego just Perform!'
Carole King's Musing * Tapestry & Neil Young's Harvest.
Golden Rushes

'Hey I gotta Jet dude'
'Our leaders know what's best' ~ realise this is bullshit!
What about elements of Personal liberty and Tolerance
that define our society? ~ We might destroy ourselves!!!
The prosecution of these wars is indefensible and we know
that we were Fully lied to and yet have accepted it. WHY?

*

'IAO' total surveillance Profile ~ very natural I'm sure!
All personal information on US citizens in a central database.
Who said honest people having nothing to hide? Prove it!
Guilty until you prove yourself Innocent, mother fuckers!
Do I get to retain my Private Life, how about my wife?
(NSA) What do you do with such an INTRUSION dad?
Look at the Paranoia and Confusion, in the UK society!
They wonder, pretend innocence for these violent crimes
and Anti-social behaviour, stalking their streets & homes.
We are living in a culture created on Fear, 'As Seen on TV'
This is your Guarantee! Sorry, No Offence....

*

Who sets what's normal in your Mind > And the Fraud?
'Online programs to read your emails and hear all phone calls...'
By law voted in by New Labour, 2000 *~ Welcome Millennium!*
Gathering Personal Info. seeing through your infra-ray firewalls.
Probes - evaluations for your Record; your Doctor, Investigator,
Benefit Agency. Threats of Advanced Computational POWER.
Is that You, 'Facial Recognition System' at the beauty salon?
80 nodal points on Your face transformed into Algorithms ~
Checked against Passports and Driving Licenses; Oh mum!
Why did you sign my birth certificate as collateral for the state?
Biometric fingerprints, instantaneous scanning & you only
came in the shop to buy spring onions, carrots & bananas.
Hidden sensors in the car tires, chips read by skimmers.
Is this in any way going to help to understand 'disorders',
depressions, syndromes, stress, nerves or make it worse?

Objective Meaning > "You Are a Little Planet"
It's hard not putting your picture to all this stuff. Flows
Bottom line ~ it's a field of energy ~ non-Identificational.
Something is happening in some 'reality', this Is Existing!
Whatever it is, Interplanetary, natural, chemical, chaos ego/less,
karma or suffering, or surreal, hallucinogenic, the jungle, Kali or Maya.
*Because 'I' in some sense is existing * on a level of body field energy.*
Field of Love, ignorance, light, sensation, feeling, whatever it is tune in.
*Relatively Yin (*)Yanging * it's essentially ~ Integrally Universal energy.*
*Holistically * being here * now in this instant * omnipresent!*
Accept, allow it ~ 'Conscious awareness of this Reality'
How you reflect Spirituality ~ being in your happy place
*

'The Things You Own, The Things Owning You'
*"I can't help that, the drugs were tools to me * microscopes.*
I used them to change my focus in various ways ~ to learn
the full potential of the human nervous system & the rest"
Acid Projection ~ but the 'Turning On' is just the first step.
The message now is that the message keeps changing.
Intelligence must increase as Consciousness expands
or we get burned-out ~ I've just wised up!
"Truth, Truth, Truth that's the highest circuit of all ~"
"They don't have to keep repeating old misery imprints
We can become immortal and go to the Stars"
*

We Are Astral Love Fields
Everything we experience is mind's finite hallucination ~ Maya
"The reality is a structural, mathematical, logical principle
we don't see. That is each person creates his own
Universe out of his own neurological processes ~
Science is nothing else but the search for the unseen,
structural integrities that underline these appearances".
Pp. 123/5. Dr. Timothy Leary. In Robert Anton Wilson's
'Cosmic Trigger, The Final Secret Of The Illuminati'

<u>*Off the Top of My (Cosmic) Trolley*</u>
*How about trying a bit of '**Unconditional Love**'…*
Keep Up your Power ~ Energy no matter what
*Your Value * Your Worth ~*
Feeling Consciously
*
<u>*Definitely Conditions of a Conspiracy*</u>
Fear + (Loathing) in the New World Order, Electronic Monitoring.
Official, Machine Environment; NSA, CIA, Mossad; Oh that one!
'Psychological Warfare' on us! (Spooks, Independent.15/2/08)
ID. chips in bins, freaking people out, Criminalising Granddad.
The template of what is determined as Normal behaviour!
'YOUR ACTIONS WILL BE DETECTED!' - Believe us!
Tracked and monitored on your way to school, to work.
In the toilet, in your bed with a global positioning device!
Comes as standard piece of kit with a Vengeance Vibrator,
CCTV; flagged in mobile phones, your car. Photo-records
Smart I cameras (but not that clever) Profiling > Programs.
<u>*You Will behave Differently*</u> *(depends what they want from us)*
To All the Rules, Regs; Taxes, By Laws, Unspecified Wars.
The Troubles, the Incidents, the Attacks on some poor sod!
Who does it benefit mate; can I still get my social benefit Guv?
Powerlessness just like the Miners & Dockers strikes in 1980's.
Even the Ending of the Planet! Civilisation as we know it ~
Global Warming doing its Dirty Deed, never your Greed,
*not Your Ignorance! No Sense of Spirit within One*self!*
Who does that Really Benefit? Keeps our Mind down low,
deep, horrible, at a Welsh, Scottish, Yorkshire Coal seam!
Is it Impossible in this way to be Truly safe? Despotic Oppressors!
It's been created and Maintained to Weaken us all & our children!
Our Power kept in Paranoia, desperate need, disease, debt, greed.
Why are we in this negative state, not freed? Don't use Codex seed!
Easily Controlled, Coerced, Ruled, Exploited, You Obey, not your say.
Easier to Separate lost and Intolerant souls. Divining not Conquering!

*Zappa's Big Tao * Out of Order*
Media (who reads the Daily Mail?) makes who Feel Unsafe?
Fear ~ of the Insanity, not even looking at who we really are!
Only seen as a Potential Victim! (look at Pensioners in the UK today)
And what is New Labour doing, it's gotten Worse, under their Control!
What happened to the Sense that we're all Inter connected ~ Socially.
It was called a Society, Cosmic integration now it's Mass Psychosis ~
Mass Unconscious, feeling susceptible to others
We don't even know....

*

State of Mind
'Paranoid' Is Just a descriptive Word
Amongst specious Materialisation not Spiritual!
Who is distorting, disordering whom my Lord?
U turning over to a field of sense consciousness
just energetic dancing Cosmic molecules ~

*

*What is this ability, creation * materialisation?*
Of a thing - of a Universe, of Stella winds,
of a Sun, of an Invisible entity
Quantum theory

*

We have
MATERIALISED
Mother Nature
Mother Nature
has created Us.
We've Identified the Carina Nebula, 8000 light years from Earth.
Solar flares, ultra violet radiation effecting, hiding polar bears!
Developed DNA; cloned fluorescent Korean caterpillar in spray.
Global warming, starving millions, disaster, Paranoia looming.
Darfur corruption, melting Ice caps, burning forests, life-death.
Ultimately Manifestation Is ~ like it or not, becoming.
Sure people do take the piss but we're here now

Saraswati & Brahma
What you thinking about
when it may never happen?
Focusing on how I feel ~
Krishna it's all him * everything!
'You are the rocket-ship of Love!'
"It's never enough for some people"
*

The Life Force
Is in the space ~
Between the atoms
Between your lips
Between his legs
Crystals sparkling in her burning bush.
Pointillism of the full Moon from Earth
Co*existence in a fantastic realm, why not?
"It's in the Allowance ~ Your Experience
Not the judgments"
*

Conversations with Ronnie Rat & Stella Ray
Animatronics, you're losing it Baba!
Those circuits ~ cloning an Objective
of desire, matey. Rooting Flora's smiles.
Cloning apples on a sprouting tree, New Evie.
Replicates ~ unnatural genitalia throbbing in heat
waves ~ thinking about it > can you really do that?
Made a 100 billion year infection from a drop of DNA.
"The sun shines freely, doesn't choose who it shines on"
*

Launch the work ~ flow
"Kept his nose clean, we like that!"
Signals from outer galaxies of no time ~
'There's lots of Space in an atom to be creative'
Electrons, protons, neurons of manifesting peace

Conceived in a Veil

Whatever you're doing, is acting as a reflective mirror of
Reality ~ (you are reality) so fully embrace its embrace.
Not 'Marketing smoke', Psychology of Mass Insanity
of Big Brother, only designed with the Viewer, in Mind!
Hooks you in bondage or see through it. A good exercise
behind the scenes as an 'Observer' of mental depression.
So not caught up in Illusion, pain, hyper-disorders of Maya.
Not caught up in the 'Matrix'; or any of the true conspiracies.
Isn't that their Aim, Control your thoughts, YOU*US*POWER!
They know some of the buttons to Push-Pull & Twist-Wrench
In your brain cells of fear, greed, obsession, delusion, dogmatism,
resentment, lust, blindest faith, deviations of the ego, ignorance, sin,
hate, guilt, denial and all those spliced genes from ancient species!
Without realising there are Innumerable 'Un/\diagnosed' known ~
unknown, behavioural, neurological, emotional, mental 'disorders',
physical diseases, 'abnormal' moods with no holistic understanding.
Spiritual harmony, compassion, witnessing realms of the unconscious.
So that we're all existing in these unnatural -ve frequency realities.
Separated, isolated, alienated from our human family tribe.
Use a clear reflection to Know thy Self; some will crash!
Break the spell, cut the strings, step back, be Objective
to the feelings in your heart, see your powerful **D**esires.
Not working by Rules striving for the Matrix's industrious hive.
Realise it's a field of Sense Consciousness in time ~ space.
Is our Planet doomed? **'This Precious Jewel in the Sky'** ~
Are you born free in the psychical web or trapped in orbit,
don't you Know? We're all wearing invisible black burkhas.
Until we walk out through the walls of our man made Prison.
I'm already living in beautiful, natural, friendly, open Goa.
Got a permaculture garden with free parties at the hill top.
Floating with my mind in the sea at noon.
Meditating on a fully lit up Shiva moon ~
Flying with shooting stars in infinite space

The Model
I have Nothing to cause problems with other egos ~
Already living creatively, inspiration and loving freely
Wonderful chilling out at the German Bakery Ashram.
Being part of an ecological sustainable community ~
to get to the beach navigate around 15 coconut trees
while a Diva plays the heavenly flute to 'Om Shanti'
Big green gathering of my laughing friends ~
Keeping the Mantra consciously in the heart.
A Buddha field beside the Arabian sea.

*

Intuitive
More synergy meditation
on nothing but awareness

*

She came on the still wind
She appeared from Solar radiation
Stars in your eyes Astral traveller
Who wrote those lines?
Their intention took you to a natural paradise.
They stayed for the monsoon always smiling.
Frequencies of Tantra love, overlooking the river
Ecstasy ~ at dawn waking together on the balcony.
Making Puja to his energetic lingam,
giving sweet, juicy fruit to her Yoni.
Screaming in the Jungle at night

*

Alternatives
Have you ever heard of 'Spiritual Democracy'?
Elites confiscating all common land by the Sea!
Astral space in your face
A child in your smile ~
'Namaste'

<u>Frozen out birds</u>
Mind splits open with butterflies & extinct dinosaurs ~
A big brown bear in a Top hat bounding into the Cosmos
carrying copies of George Battaille's, 'Story of the Eye'
Nabakov's hyper existential 'Invitation to a beheading'
'Karma Control just as evil since our eternal damnation
leaves the starving, wretched behind, lying in the ditch'
You never know; 'Sun shines out their arse' that's Rich
& Marriage dispels the delusion, divorce comes later!
I've just broken up! Might use it for a screenplay...

*

<u>Skin that you deserve</u>
A Rich White American, Male Christian Straight ~
How come they have the Power? (so they believed)
Easy Karma, to accept the one dimensionality...
Looking in the Past, looking in the Future ~
only thing that exists is this Cosmic Instant
is the eternity now but You have to Realise it!
Ultimate Avatar * Eternity is happening right now.
Transparent Karma, a tool controlling the Masses.
Controlling the flow in you ~ putting you in a BOX
with bars of holy psychology; look out for neurosis!
You don't have the answer, they say they do. No doubts!
Giving you guilt complexes that you need them to forgive.
Kill your Ego so we can insert our own Brain Detergent,
Propaganda Programs, belief systems, religious morality!
Face it, holding it to Yourself, looking at it all Objectively.
Thinking it's coming from the Outside, find Your Inner Guru

*

<u>Dharavi Mumbai Slum</u>
Being really thankful for what you have ~
Never forget that Mr. Superstitious, Karmic Philosopher.
So this slum is never going to end; Congress Ordained!
Is it so unbelievable that one million people 'exist' here?

How to let it flow with different people's egos?
More open is less control. How will it grow in his heart?
Such a cool vibe ~ what did you expect?

*

Dark Matter
You are existing ~
Energy field is present
Field of sense consciousness
Beingness

*

At*om Boom*Shanka!
Don't be a slave
to your hair!
Does your Mind
have a Mind of its own?

*

Gerhard Richter Extracts (New Tate 26:10:07)
"Visualises a Reality which we can neither see nor
describe but which we may nevertheless conclude
to exist" ~ suggesting invisible 'states of flux'
Demonstrates Inventiveness (is that free spirit?).
Cutting magazines, word arrangement, found objects.
Abstract film is Not Reality. Art Objects becoming ~
Integral elements of Pictorial language.
A rhythm of cubist Planes
Pure Abstraction, layout of page,
Imbuing with Pure Pleasure too.
"Cubism shattered Illusions of the canvas
As a view onto the World ~
Collages of memory, synchronicity of poetics"
"Grey is suitable for Illustrating nothing,
*doesn't trigger off feelings*associations…*
Resistance to Ideologies ~ Non Attachment
to Design"

King Blood
"I think Krishnamurti said, it was all shit.
It's the 'human moment' not the human!
As soon as you Think it, put a name to it,
You're not doing it, that's not Meditation".
..."To name it God, is to Kill Your God"
Meditation is Nothing we can describe
Beyond thought ~ we can experience it;
It's Limitless, in the first place.
Biology falling from the Stars
*

Spacey flowers of Life
Everyone with 'No Mind' into hyper Quantum infinity
Macro*Micro Quarks, silly strings in Sacred geometry.
Napoleon for the boys, Mary Magdalene for the girls.
Nuclear guns blasting right through 'Vous', les Cathars!
Choices, give it for good luck, bouncing into 'Dolce Vita'
Keeping it light didn't need another population burnt
to death because they believed in non-violence & herbs
but a Pope gave you the box of matches!
*

White Magic
No brain, no thoughts, Mind in free flight ~
When the beginning of a day appears from night.
Just hope it's not in a valley running downhill, being
chased by nearly extinct, upset, tree climbing Grizzlies.
Messed with another community and got the results!
They're not cannibals, only interested in Food not You.
Direct to the source, allow yourself to fall into the Stars.
'Maya' ~ Illusion all in your head; You are the Heavens!
Can't be that simple, but it is.
A Tunnel or Universal vision darling, full of radiant light!
"You're on Your Yoni" a lovely wonderful sight
"I did pass out"

New para * dime shift
Please leave me in Boynton or Bell Canyon with the Vortices.
Not selling your mother or selling your nature for a red cent!
Selling you an angle of Capitalism after Africans sold their own
neighbours as slaves & Romans fed their lions Christian chops!
'Appearance of freedom with reality of control' *said Dr. Leary.*
'Floors in Las Vegas are imperceptibly slanted for gravity
to pull you down into the playing pit'. That's some level ~
of Consciousness.
*

Not the Content but the Context
"Biological Imperative that's all we're looking for ~
to be eaten by a woman, preferably big tits, wet lips"
Very complex insects in there
"You have to impress me"
Sexy Starfish
*

Ossiary
'Kutnah Ora' (Cathedral of bones)
end of the Cold War
"when they all fucked off"
*

"I never saw her face"
Transmuting, transcending Our Mind! Ourselves ~
Don't you think you can escape that idea?
hanging out doing his Spider thing!
Cog 366, "Put me in the wood chipper face first"
A fear of being penniless, don't really matter.
No Plans, go with the process, flow ~
Cleansing the Reality of Death.
"Nobody happens after we die" * Atman's flying sky high.
Above a bunch of Egoists ~ Onward journey into eternity
You don't even have to die to get there
Exactly Shiva ~ I AM NOW

'Truth Poses a Threat to Power'
'The bigger the lie the more People believe it.' Anonymous.
Are our Eyes telling us the Truth? Chemical Interconnections.
Brain's getting lots of Info, in frequency ~ vibratory wave bands
we can't filter, Realise it all, so! How do You Perceive?
How do we know that your blood is red and not blue?
Dualist separation of fig leaves & apples from Paradise.
Dark energy Universe is mostly empty. What 'Reality' is Unseen?
You cannot see the official papers for 75 years! National Security:
Evidence of a Coup d'état available in 2038 or that assassination!
And $80 Billion on Militarised Escalation of Iraqi Conflict?
"If the Government Murders Truth It Murders its People"
*

Have you been to Tibet? Yeah, I've got a Visa for China!
In a short Space of Time, the waking & dreaming World.
Probably got a brand new Walmarts in Tianneman Square.
A Pirated Starbucks roasting at the exclusive Potala Palace.
Being a traveller; outside the Control of tyrants is a Luxury.
"Indians were quite happy fighting amongst themselves".
Which country never had war, conflicts, & disagreements?
'History is rarely written by the Conquered' - not in Gaelic!
Who controls Popular Media; the dictates of Education?
Found Painted stories in Medieval Stained Glass windows.
Lots of thought into Protecting their Territory of Lion farms!
*

New drone over Bethlehem
Pancho pill, buzz kill Overshadowing….
Cigarette Sheriff, Sugar Mama & Bufo Toad!
"Male desires it ~ Female desires to be it"
Hooking up to a different program, serving hot women.
"Vertical roast beef sandwiches coming up from the hips"
Securing borders of fear with a Peace Wall of No Colour!
Force fields of aura, taking M16s from the glazed children.
Taking the Violence out from their Minds and Hearts ~

For Starters
A Melanoma Fruit Salad with burnt cream.
Melting back into that black hearted woman
Dark Magic's pulsating essences on Ruby lips ~
Attracting vibrant Yonis for Cosmic Reproductions
*

'The Painted Bird'
Chimping monkeys sitting in a circle grunting, "Have mercy!"
Carnal tongues sucking blue lingams in Spiral Cunilingus
on fleshy, flapping membranes, dude there's a Spaceship!
Monitoring - came to pick us up! No it's a weather balloon
Even Uncle Ho was voted in; Captain of a Petrol Tanker
Let the Thunderbird, Raven, Fox, other Spirit guides take
tortured, screaming victims on flights into Heaven's dells.
*

Cultures of Miss selling everything & Stealth Extortion
There is a Statue to Boris Yeltsin in Catania, Sicily, Italy.
There's A Monument to Tony Blair beside the River Styx
And a Shrine to George Bush & Cronies in Damnation
& a Portrait of Genghis Khan by Nixon's in the Pentagon.
Kissinger's & Pinochet's ashes spread in a Reich bunker.
Mao's name can never be spoken in any village of Tibet.
All Assassins You should be very fearful of eternity ~
Warning to all you New Despots & Genocidal Maniacs
*

Not to Fight ~ to be natural
Transcending Psychedelic Mind; above the lime green clouds
of Santiago. Castaneda's early writing * Surreal Dali's vision!
"If You Fear Death You Fear Everything In This World"
Only the Ego will be Freaked!
Breathing In Breathing Out & the Silence
"Rhythm is the Mother Tongue"
"It's God making contact with Itself"
"You have to be Open to be ~ free"

No Knowing
I'm always interested in people's behaviour, darling ~
Shiva*Shakti's honey moon, I figured it out for myself;
Psychic Psychedelic Ergot bonbons with bluish auras.
Velvety expression between her veils, under the Pyramid.
"This estimate would not Include Squaws taken for Concubinage
Neophytes were charged with Sorcery" Official Korean history.
"Why does it have to be Your way only?"
Concentric ~ Pointing to Stars in the Heavens

*

La Bio*luminescent Fleuve
Flashes & Splashes *Whizzing around inside the body.
How does such a person come into the Limelight? With
such an obscure, unheard knowledge ~ Synchronous clash.
For one discovered famous as Yogananda, many are unknown.
Gurus watching Himalayan pink, ruby, magenta, indigo Sunrises.
"When we kissed in the Temple." "I kissed you first ~

*

Navigators Beyond the Window
And what about what you don't know?
What about what you might know one day
What about what you will know one day
What about what you'll never know
And might never want to know?
Two way mirrors ~ the other side of your conscience.
Now ~ Opening it all up, crossing over the flat-horizon.
Discovers, Spirit explorers sailing on the river of Time

*

Mer = light Ka = spirit Ba = physical body
"Shift your consciousness & restore the memory
of the Infinite possibilities of your existence ~
Using this tool will bring an automatic field of protection.
Programming Your 'Body of Light' to Create Your Life
As a Perfectly balanced Being"

Flowers of Life
'Place the Merkaba Yantra so that the centre is at
the level of the third eye (middle of the forehead).
Use it as an open eye meditation target. Gaze at
the centre of the Yantra without blinking (Tratak).
Breathe it into your Mind and allow with the out ~ breath
that it expands & surrounds your body. Fill it up with light
Shift the Centre of your Merkaba from the Solar Plexus ~
3rd chakra to the Heart chakra ~ 4th dimension conscious.
Trust that your Intention has activated your Merkaba'
Learning to accept, Intuitional being, Taoism season.
Don't know the scientific meaning of 'Quantum'
but ok with the feeling ~ it's being channelled

*

How do you want to Love me?
Reflections of the Mind
Reflections from beyond the Mind
Reflections on Your Mind
Reflections from your heart
Feelings in your heart
Plant a wild flower garden, summer meadow.
Together on a dusky belvedere in Sienna
with morning glories blazing at the dawn

*

'Refi'
'Roll up all your debts into one'. "As seen on TV"
Slogans so easy, it's no big deal! Unified a Sin.
Losing information using your information all illegally,
Metadata, Raw Information ~ broke the hypnosis' spell…
The UK. Government lost 25 million Personal files in Nov/2007.
In London misplaced a laptop with 600,000 Personnel data files.
Includes Bank, Passport, National Insurance, National Health
records of serving members of the Armed Forces! (1/19/2008).
Corruption, criminal negligence who is ever held responsible?

Renaissance Dawn
Face to face in pure nature ~ Kites in the air
Living in a forest glade outside Piacenza.
Turning off the brain-dictator.
Floating off the Mind
Floating off the bow
Turning off the gas ~
Jungle Tigers prowling into extinction!
Transmissions ~ "Be on it or Bin it"
"What is Liquid Crystal?"
'Live & Laugh'
*

Endless Fun
Lovely Ocean sea breeze, her constituents in Hawaii.
Making deeper contemplation on the Kusala Sankharas.
Good tendencies tend to arise ^ being a happy person ~
Doctrine of origination, simultaneously & interdependently.
No fear of death, just a process of dying ~ is it destiny?
Highest wisdom is connecting to the law of change.
Death won't seem unnatural
Ultimate origin of things
1st cause is Unthinkable ~ Beginningness
*

I was hoping ~ she would have done it of
her own free will, not an adrenalin junkie!
The Mind is Selfish ~ Self-fulfilment.
Liberation from it * letting go of her.
Kissing you on the Bridge of Sighs ~
Your Mind for now is running the show.
You have come to the Place
where nothing is hidden ~
Left the Long March ~ 'Trail of Tears'
for the pathless path of joy and wisdom

Sure > < "Protect Yourself from White Marks"
Bullshit "If you don't Mind, it don't really matter"
"Energy that could be flowing to Higher ground"
Limiting our exposure to all the violence
to my fellow swimmers in Cosmic streams
We are the ones we've been waiting for ~
Always recognised by our own heart
Remembering that we are all One, at least Quantum.
Separation is fear ~ energetic recognition, condition.
How fit is your Mind's Program, of its Intention to be?
Need to get some Spiritual Supra devotional strategies...
Death is a Great Leveller; Love the greatest Inspiration.
"Release the habit of the habit of the pain of pain ~
The gift of Timeless wisdom is always recognised
by our own hearts
*

Not playing in your game Caesar
Systems and goals of dysfunctions, ask Socrates.
Ask Gurus sitting on the shore to angels of Venus.
Meditation on: 'Death will take place' for a start.
Meditation on ~ Cosmic beingness in your heart.
With you in the celestial summer of blissful ecstasy.
Delight can come at any moment
*

Earth Wind Fire & H2O*Right Contemplation
Free from craving ~ conscious at that moment
In any form of existence, Mindful is awareness
of Impermanence, not unnerved gives you Reality.
Take the 'Voyage of Discovery of Truth and respect'
Not the weakness of disinclination to understanding
the ego's Ignorance, distractions of the Human Mind.
It is what it is, I am as I am; a mango falling from a tree.
Law of Gravity, the nature of things; Not living in
a fool's paradise ~ Each weaves their own web

Icing on Top
"My Religion of Love"
"the candle that ever burns ~
It's the person you are; people who've enriched my life"
*

<u>*Saying, "Where ignorance is bliss it is folly to be wise"*</u>
"Beings are the Oneness of their deeds"
'Life and death ~ Rise and fall of a holistic tree'
We are already enlightened potential, It is in us.
The flame of the Universe burns alive in us ~
Don't be distracted and confused or deluded
A reflective Mind asks what is the cause of death?
'Disease ~ the irregular function of the human system'
It's clear as mud, be the mud, being muddy mud with Lotus.
Life force in the stone, an insect, plants, beingness here now
Breathing Prana
*

<u>*Healinghereandnow.com*</u>
The Merkaba is an energy field of light that surrounds
our body. It's built of two Tetrahedrons (male & female)
creating a Star Tetrahedron that has three aspects.
The Primary aspect always remains stationary while
the other two aspects rotate in different directions.
Creating this energy field of light and unconditional love
has been practised in the Mystery schools of Lemuria
Atlantis and Egypt as a tool of ascension.
It is part of Sacred Geometry ~
which purpose is to show 'the Unity'.
<u>*Effects and benefits:*</u> *'Meditation on the Merkaba Yantra*
will operate the 4th Chakra ~ Your Heart and connect you
with Universal Love. It will activate your 'Body of Light' ~
'The Merkaba' and strengthen your ability to work with
your energetic field. Once your Merkaba is activated
you will have expanded awareness of who you are

'Iraq Survey Group' - His Conclusions

I have to do nothing to express myself, natural independence.
Couldn't open their mouths, talking on giant mushroom clouds!
Is there any Justification for anyone to go to War?
Beingness Is a Blessing.
'Might Makes Right' bro, at least to Genghis Khan and crew!
You're either with US or Against US; that's Real Democracy!
'Iraq is a diversion to Terrorism' Liberating it for Colonialism!
Their 'Axis of Evil' Bush's Toolbox, such brutal Instruments!
We Know it's All Lies, Lost the United Nations in the process,
seen as weak, unfortunately no power to stop another genocide.
No power but great careers for boys/gals at top of the food chain!
It's a very bad joke they told you to shut up & be quiet or else!
Everyone knows it was set up, a game but good job prospects.
And You All knew there were no WMDs, didn't stop good ol' USA!
Powell 2/2001 >"he has no weapons, no capability"< 7/2001 Rice.
Extending empathy to a future with Codex Alimentarius seeds & trees.
He doesn't need any more Acid, he's used up all his gift tokens.
'Attached to our Roles & our Poles' who's seeing you as you are?
'I want to get in touch with my fabulous nature ~'
"It's You who will define when you say the word 'I'"
"Wealth should be the ability to be generous"
Competition lazy fare; Between man & woman
And the man & woman in each of us.
"Enlightenment is bullshit, like a product sold to you"
"It's not outside yourself, if they tell you it is, it's a lie"
"like turning up at a Clam Rally in a Boy George outfit."
The town was bombed 18 months straight; Reality check!
The living proof, a living legend.
We're all Universal babes
Partying since the Stone age, bad old days, burnt Evelyn at the stake!
Chopped off another consort's noggin, no goin' back ~ it's all within.
Life is being in fields of energy, can I have some water please?
"I don't make any rules Dick, I go with the flow"

<u>Called Them Bogus</u>
Where's Salvador Dali or Henry Miller when you need them?
News teams, readying their troops for Iraq War 19/3/2003.
Raw Intel Advocating it, Desensitising their Population!
Same old game worked a treat on the British under Blair.
One sided Patriotism of a Fascist, New Labour 'Democracy'
Thumbs up, "To kill the message kill the True messenger."
Selectively taking info; distortions, fake, complete nonsense.
5/2/2003 Powell presents his false 'Credibility' to the World!
Biological ordnance factories found in artist's renditions, manga tales!
World Wide Web of Deceit, none of it true from any of these specimen!
Up to his neck in carnage/death, on his way to his place in Hell.
Got them from the Pentagon, Rumsfeld gave them all Weapons!
*

UN Inspectors right all the time, no weapons, just a Ruse!
Media's in bed with the Government, Info fed from Pentagon.
No evidence review; Anthrax shelf life, three years from 1994.
500 tons of Saran and VX, shelf life two months; now 12 yrs old!
No Nuclear weapons, 'Warped Intelligence', Political Corruption,
on a Criminal scale, should be tried as Crimes Against Humanity,
sedition, treason, Capital offence, abusing their positions of Trust!
Straight Lies to the Nation, the World, ain't No 'al -Qa'ida' either!
Scare tactics to exploit the Fear; trauma of Americans since 9/11.
Destroying any Trust, the Foundation of any real relationship.
USA/UK. you've completely dishonoured yourself in the eyes of us all.
*

<u>Lost All Credibility with your Fake Yellow Cake</u>
'African Uranium' - UK 'Intel' from a 'groomed defector'.
Criminal to present lies to Congress again, another patsy.
Secretary Rice had her suspicious doubts about a forgery!
Oh Yeah! Nothing Authentic; they checked out of Reality.
War Fever took over on Capitol Hill; didn't mind giving
false testimony for $1 million from a Barbaric Regime!
Now how can you tell other Tyrants to abide by the law?

Pali: Sam 'together', Kar 'to make', combined together.
"Death has no fears for those protected by Dhamma"
"All things in this world are aggregates ^ combinations,
they do not exist by themselves" Holistic, Cosmic Gaia
Interconnected ~ nothing is one entity, only a concept
*of our senses * 'One Infinity' ~ 'Permanence' gives Pain!*
Sequencing of thoughts arising, remaining, passing away.
A Rapidity, an Illusion of permanence ~ being called Mind.
Only a stream of thoughts (consciousness) passing away.
'River is only a name, it's just a flow, changing energies ~
where to go? "There is No experience but the experience,
there is no doer but the deed", says Anatta, ultimately ~
"There is No Nature or Person who dies just the Process"
Less attached, less Identifying ~ ourselves with our actions,
with our 'disorders'. This is the 'Abhidhamma' view of things.
Energetic, Illumination, Liberation, Revelation, Life processing.
*So No stress, disorder, fears or Ego < * > Nothing really dies ~*
*

*Soul is *beingness* is Soul*
"No such thing as 'Permanent' Mind
It's just a stream of thoughts ~
Life is changing every moment
Nothing is permanent in Reality.
*Man's Psyche*physical combination (nama/rupa)*
As the light of knowledge dispels the darkness."
'Mind' does Not Exist in Reality; how about that?
That's really like pulling a white rabbit out of a hat!
*

'So accustomed to the delusion, habit of Identifying, judging
ourselves with our Image, our actions; breeding grounds of
dualistic EGO ~ It's just the Mind's reactions to Objects.
When we walk it's just a process of walking (no soul).
A fallacy of something within us directing it, thinking!
No one there who suffers, just a Process of 'dukkha!'

*Intergalactic Magic * Cobalt Blue Glitter Lights*
Eyes of a Hawk ~ Welcome Intergalactic flying Horus.
Not the Ultra-Genetic surveillance of a Genome Project.
Accepted by society, lost in a desert, killing your demons.
Risky data bases hard to control < Orchestration!
Unlike Eliza Markova ~ ballet defying Gravity

*

Society of the Surveillance Generation
Microchips scanned from inside your face & Skin ~
Technology Dev! Information of a Brave New World
Crazy things become acceptable in your digital house!
We're belonging to environments of Interactive response
Smart floors, smart ceilings, smart Invasions, smart eyes.
Wraparound apathy smart control, smart unaccountable
Organisations, smart education, smart Beliefs & faiths!
Those holding the Power, "In a Wilderness of Mirrors"
50 million web-cams in US. in 2004! Balance of Control?
Transponders, Implanted Silicon chips, Computer Systs!
Transferring digital, human thoughts ~ electronic signals.
Frequency on our way to being Cyborgs, Biological Machine.
GPS. Satellites, 'Being Watched All the Time', Why do it?
"We Accept Intrusions that once seemed Impossible…
Into the Invisible Network, No Alarm!
Spilling Isolated menstrual blood

*

Broken Devotion
Despising all the negatives
Bad Karma in your smile ~
Coming across the Sunset alive…
flamingos migrating to Lake Nakuru.
You cooked the lot….
for a change
'Sacred' ~ I like that word
Looking for inspiration in fields of Stargazer lilies

Just a Process the rest is a Delusional, Mad Concept

"No one dies it's just a process of dying ~ no fear, suffering.
Not identifying with bodily and Mental functions so No Ego
delusions; beingness is complete detachment of the Mind"
I see thousands of bees & one mosquito heading this way!
Thinking that within us something thinks is a fallacy, a movie!
Just the dying, there is no one, no ego there to die, bro!
CLARITY OF A DYING PROCESS ~ STREAMING PROCESS
Slow down get a clear reflection of this 'Illusion of Mind'
Changes the rules and vision of the World, it's transitory.
'Anicca' ~ no permanence, Quantum is moving everything.
Me a Processing Time Machine with Pan at the wheel!

*

Make a New Energy Meditation

*There's not too much * there's not enough*
pushing up the daisies, growing in the moment
I had six black years! Seize that moment of revelation.
Interpretation of a Relative Manifestation
Remembering something that makes you laugh ~
Looking at it in a different way, change your perception.
"It took me years to get depressed and more years to unravel it!"
Admitting it yourself, seeing your own mind's creating this movie!
And what do you like? Which caricature is wearing your mask?
Try reprogramming yourself to be happy, finding a new Dolche vita.
Ask the monk who sold his old Ferrari, that is worth an unknown price.
"I'm healthy, dynamic and fully alive!" Curing myself or killing myself!
There's a few stepping stones to get here and it's not over to the last one.
Who is believing in what the facts show. How about a loveless marriage?
Who the fuck is happily married? 'Happy wife, happy life'- allegiance.
Suffer the consequences, you just can't say that on the doorstep.
Had me arrested for wanting to see my daughter!
I want to live in a Temple the rest of my life....
Kissing trees and eating Sunlight

Tapping Collective Unconscious
Writing a poem
Singing a song
dancing a dance
with Life with Love with you
to travel ~ forget the past
now ~ streams of consciousness
A poet's ~ Elixir living in Tunefulness.
'Let us make Human in our own image.'
Polytheists don't even need the wave ~
"You make stuff up it has to be believable.
It's called the 'Suspension of disbelief'"
360° of my thought process

*

Want to build an Empire, find a Jesuit in a Catacomb!
A Genesis, "Your Instincts have to usurp your emotions ~
Emotions overcoming your biological imperative."
That's what we want, "Jesus was a fiction", Holy Land too?
'Inshallah' theme parks for Religious Zealots; Dodgems Drive.
Omnificent Pharaoh, why should we worship you as God?
"The Church is the oldest Global Corporation in the World"
A total Con; does the Pope know? Of course, they all do!
Thrown all the Christians to the Lions! Unbelievably ~
First acid trip finding your Infinity, losing your virginity.
Two way mirrors, learnt so much from the conspiracy stream.
Everything's coming from the Collective sub-conscious ~
Outside/Inside when you look in a mirror what do you see?
A reflection of Yourself, "I just wanna go to Heaven baby!"
Each time different, shooting energy bolts out of her head.
"I didn't know she had a sword until she busted it out!"
Why must people follow a formula, Hieronymus Bosch?
Dali flies in a Moon of Honey on your Martyrdom video -
Your name will be carried on in your DNA *ireal seeds.
"We're the only animals that fuck face to face"

95

British Spartans
"I like birds best" seeing my lovely sense of nostalgia ~
"Charged with the unlawful possession of your suitcase"
that's when you're ordered what to do; do you still want it?
"Champignons in a tin, nothing but the best for Palmer"
like yesterday, 'the Swinging 60's', so dated, so sedated,
they won't open to new life, maintaining the old controls.
Authorities, rules & regulations in all aspects, censoring
getting a sense of today's culture v corruption, racism v
Immigration debate, read the Daily Mail for a taste of it!
We kill more, faster, quicker; Legitimated trials in Iraq!
Might have been driven stark, ravin' Mad, time of the #6,
'The Prisoner', 'Man from Uncle' Cold War era Paranoids.
More deaths than any film or computer game, how real?
Blame it on the weather, new tropical bugs or something,
being globally cool with fun fetishes & mystical meditations
On undiscovered coral beaches ~ with shoals of angel fish.

*

This Is The N E W S
Everybody to be in a continual nightmare!
You see the Love within * Not the Darkness.
"You're not gonna move back in so you can fuck off
And you're not gonna see the kids!"
I certainly wouldn't do it if I had to watch out for Babylon.
When you're mangled you become a caricature, living in a cartoon.
Everyone turned into a duck, 'quack, quack, quack, quack, quack!'
"We are the Revolution, we've Stopped doing what we're told."
Leaving Planet Earth, alright until I got to the door, cocaine poisoning!
Rewiring the sperm in your bollocks for the task to come!
Imitating the complexities of Nature ~
No one knows what's going on really!
Give my Love to Krishna

Fundamentalist Hormones

You Can't always be spiritual or compassionate or be ~
able to care for your old parents, or dedicate your*self.
Have to give yourself space & time and know your ego.
Making a vow (consciously?) "to love & honour another
person in sickness and in health until death us do part"
Don't make your*self a guilty prisoner in a box, or her!
Can't always Identify in Buddha or Krishna's philosophy.
Need a sense of freedom to break the Iron chains of Will,
determination of a Zealot to take it All too seriously dear!
"I am Sujata, please take rest and have refreshment Sir"

*

Venus Cream

Chasing Diana to a forest glade ~
Chasing a dragon into the stream
Sky pilot with Psy*chics in hot pursuit.
"And I was blessed blissed"
One drop went on a sugar lump…
Saw me going out of my body ~ later
Astral projections, holograms inside your fractal brain.
I managed to get my shoes off & my head went 'Twang'
"Don't fight it Feel it"

*

The Best Tattoo

Blew all her circuits ~ fried her brain into a cinnamon roll.
"You have to let go of everything you hold on to normally."
Then the person transmutes ~ transcends to end of timelessness.
Still hanging with the Images; surrendering means losing control,
do it consciously ~ 'I am this boundless beingness'
Beautiful turquoises of Free Will, doing what we do ~
People being themselves, everything has its time, turn ~
turn, turn do it another way, there's never too much juice!
Soft, wet, velvet vulvas, too much amazing fun.
Celebration of suffering in devoted gratitude

The Prana will always put you back into your body,
or for sure you will be different, "not judgemental"
Is it good or is it bad, trust, trust, to trust ~
It's all there anyhow clear agreement to go further.
Giving the Space to Recognize themselves
Pushing them too far ~ they judge your bliss
Reflecting giving them what they miss, so long,
basically ~ themselves, everything is in the flow.
You have to give it water for the flower to grow.
Just hold the frequency ~ it's a 24 hr. Roundabout
Making the party, right now ~
'You are the party'

*

Government is to Take up the slack, not cut out all slack!
All the Ego games, Images of being Someone Special.
But Hey Ho everyone is Special
I Vibrates at the Crown Chakra.
U is the ground chakra
A is Heart, Open Heart
Work with it, bring it in..
The feeling in the emotion
over your will and attention.
Change them, feel it directly.
Feeling disharmony over your sound ~
Movement with the vibration, hearing it, dancing it ~
Transformed, broke apart, building up the free Space
of no resistance, no bondage, no attachment barriers.
Confirm that they're there living with the Trust to Open up.
Integrating nature's 'disorders' into normal life, in the light.
Allowing them to unfold, going beyond Mind's limited Form.
Creating that Space & make the Revolution ~
for healing each butterfly effecting the planet

Greenhouses of the Pleiades
Living in a toughened glass Pyramid.
To choose a path with most Heart ~
Inner beat of Intuitive feelings to feel
what is Intangibly, visceral, ephemeral
or whatever ultimately gives it meaning.
More conscious than Instinct ~ following
F U L F I L L M E N T
becoming fully human in invisible space.
In touch with the archetype of the Self ~
from flowing with the seasons of the Tao
*

Our Journey
It was the conjugal Union of all times ~
Conscious awareness, Pilgrimage of Self…
Access to All Collective Sub-conscious Areas.
Recall carries feeling of your intimate caresses.
Reconnecting, rebirthing with Spiritual Source
experiencing different concepts of Time.
Nourishing, nourishing, nourish…
*

Kairos An om in us
The Unsaid Is Known ~ Action Is No Action
Is actually the action, allowing the action to Unfold.
Participation in Time ~ engrossed losing track…
*Feel one with * not Separate, isolated, alienated*
from your original, true Self, the Tao
Getting back in touch with now ~
"The Gate of Love is always open"
Invitation looking Inward
Generosity of the freedom from fear.
Aware of being connected ~
with the underlying pattern of
Oneness with the Universe

New Baby
"Your future's arrived!"
*Cosmic * Crystal Alien*
What Is Universal
Is what's here now
Being In Love
*

Alien Speak
"Bla Bla Bla, Blu Blu Blu ....."
If You want to give yourself that Reality
You can have it: If You don't Want that Reality
You shouldn't have to have it. Amen!"
What You Choose is What You Get…
Don't be caught by the 'carrot on a stick' temptation!
Live by doing what you like right now as a foundation.
Cosmic Transmissions
"Allowance Processing"
Formed but just have to Realise it for Yourself.
The Pictures You throw out are very Important.
If You fall in the Fear You give Yourself trouble!
To hold this frequency ~
Transmuting the whole thing through light.
Showing the Whole Maya illusion through Us.
*

Discernment
The Experience ~
Is there to allow You
to Realise the differences
through our Judgments.
Learning in this duality
growing in the moment
Pressed into a diamond
Shining as a Crystal
Human being

Hanuman * Superman
You'll need diamonds to keep them!
Threw his Mala in the Sea.
"He can see everyone because he's in everyone"
"He can see You * You can't see him"
The non-self within the Self.
Shiva conquered his Ego ~
The Cobra represents 'False Ego'
Worn as jewellery, an adornment round his neck.
Sitting on the Tiger skin of his conquered passion.
Yogi in a Shiva like state.

*

Dark Moon Mystic
Shamanic knowledge ~
Love symbolises Cosmic Power
Sacrifice, humbleness, devotion, forgiveness.
Enlightened by Vedanta; pure flowing Ganga.
End of intellectual Knowledge ~ No Mind
Flowing in you like a river ~ Siddhartha.
Up & down, impermanent quantum ~ from Space.
The Cosmos is beyond the senses of Mind's limited Forms.
What is outside Mind's concepts is emptiness, free of thought.
Maya tries to come into us with temptation & 'disorder'.
Dependent on an illusory, gravitational snake ~
You really need to find the intrinsic Yourself
not someone else; meeting your hologram.
Trapped with Eve, given understanding.
Spreading seeds of Love-Apple trees
merging in Spiritual dimensions

*

The Biggest Puzzle
Is who Am I?
It's a game ~
'Who the Fuck...

<u>Take charge of Super Ego</u>
"Body is a chariot, Mind is the reins ~
Horses are the 5 senses, Intellect the driver.
Make friends with it, feeding it, healthy 'detached' food for thought!
No negativities, chaos can enter; smooth sailing on the Reality river.
Programming ~ bio-feedback scan of a conquering, Genghis Khan!"
*

<u>The Earth Is A Living Being</u>
"Death through Pleasure ~
Losing the Highest Treasure?
A Man Made biological Weapon.
Cold hearted person is a 5* Reptile!
For you an invasion is nothing to do with Karma.
'You're a destroyer or a Weapon of the destroyer!'
Big Time Invasion Plans, Heavy Metal in Nagaland.
Material Mind's gone haywire!" Once naturally, tribally free
*

<u>Story of young Sita singing Soul songs</u>
Wanting to exist in Spirituality not Matrix complexity.
Opening to the Planets * Orbiting in your eyes.
Should have known better, "Tell me Why?"
Helen on a fast ship to Troy, sailing with a delusional boy.
Sita waiting for the arrival of her Celestial King Saviour.
He had to keep his Promise, 14 years with Saturn.
Healing her broken wing ~
*

<u>Visualise his boat, visualise his family</u>
You don' have to do anything, that's the beauty.
Being truly home this is not a dream dreaming.
The Real dream, you can taste the African fruits.
Deepest Allowance, how selfish are your fears ~
You can't Kill anyone anyway; can't live in it forever.
Spirits are leaving their bodies, "bye bye darling!"
Same chemicals, Life force ~ Consciousness left

Upanishad
"Fetch me a fruit of a Banyan tree." "There is one sir"
"Break it." "I have broken it sir." "What do you see?"
"Very tiny seeds sir." "Break one" "I have broken one"
"What do you see now?" "Nothing sir." "My child" the
father said, "what you do not perceive is the essence,
and in that essence the mighty Banyan tree exists.
Believe me my child, in that essence is the self
of all that is. That is the True, that is the self ~"

*

'Cosmic Trigger Final Secret of The Illuminati'
by Robert A. Wilson > from the Ancient Babylonian p.3.
"It was the sad time after the death of the fair young god
of spring, Tammuz. The beautiful goddess Ishtar, who loved
Tammuz dearly followed him to the halls of eternity, defying
the demons who guard the Gates of Time. But at the first gate,
the guardian demon forced Ishtar to surrender her sandals,
which the wise men say symbolises giving up will.
And at the second Gate, Ishtar had to surrender her
jewelled anklets, the wise say means giving up Ego.
And at the third Gate she surrendered her robe,
which is the hardest of all because it's giving up Mind itself.
And at the fourth Gate, she surrendered her breast cups,
which is giving up the sex role.
And at the fifth Gate she surrendered her necklace,
which is giving up the rapture of illumination.
And at the sixth Gate she surrendered her earrings
which is giving up Magick. And finally at the seventh Gate,
Ishtar surrendered her thousand petalled crown
which is giving up Godhead. It was only thus,
naked that Ishtar could enter eternity."

ABOUT SUNNY JETSUN

Inspired by the sixties Sunny started traveling the world in 1970.
His spiritual journey on the hippie trail to India took him through ~
San Francisco, Los Angeles, London, Amsterdam, Paris, Vancouver,
Sidney and Kathmandu to Varanasi. His arrival on the sub-continent ~
was the beginning of writing autobiographical verses capturing his travel
experiences, encounters with remarkable people and his quest for self-
realization. Combining experimentation with drugs, sex, rock & roll, art,
meditation, Love and life in general. Sunny started to open up to a multi-
dimensional Universe. He lived the mantra, "Turn on, tune in, drop out"
realising Mind's-illusions, inspired by deeper feelings of holistic nature,
empathy*energy & Space.

Over four decades Sunny has written and published 28 books of poetry,
created over one hundred paintings, traveled the World and considers
his masterpiece to be his daughter. He has spent the past fifteen years
in Goa, India inspired by the freedom to experience and idealism of
human consciousness.

Sunny Jetsun books and art are available on the web at:

Website: www.sunnyjetsun.com
Facebook: www.facebook.com/sunnyjetsun
Amazon: www.amazon.com/author/sunnyjetsun
Smashwords: www.smashwords.com/profile/view/sunnyjetsun

.